Contents

Chairing the Board

Revised Edition

A Practical Guide to Activities and Responsibilities

John Harper

KoganPage

London Philadelphia New Delhi

Publisher's Note

Every possible effort has been made to ensure that the information contained in this book is accurate at the time of going to press, and the publishers and authors cannot accept responsibility for any errors or omissions, however caused. No responsibility for loss or damage occasioned to any person acting, or refraining from action, as a result of the material in this publication can be accepted by the editor, the publisher or any of the authors.

Indian Edition 2010

Kogan Page India Private Limited
4737/23 Ansari Road,
Daryaganj
New Delhi 110 002

This edition is for sale in the Indian subcontinent only. Not for export elsewhere.

ISBN : 978-81-7554-606-6

Published by Vinod Vasishtha for Kogan Page India Private Limited,
4737/23, Ansari Road, Daryaganj, New Delhi 110 002.

Printed and bound in India.

Notes on contributors

Michael Mander is chairman of HS Publishing Group plc and of Book Data. He is also a non-executive director on the board of Southnews plc and a member of the advisory board of WIRE Ltd. He is also involved in a number of voluntary activities in the public domain.

Michael has gained a wealth of business experience in many companies both large and small, principally in the publishing and media sector, where he has worked in the roles of chairman, chief executive, executive and non-executive director.

Sir Nigel Mobbs is chairman of Slough Estates plc, a large commercial property and development company listed on the London Stock Exchange with business operations in the UK, the United States, Canada and continental Europe. He is also chairman of Bovis Homes Group plc and a non-executive director of Barclays Bank plc, both of which companies are listed on the LSE. He is also engaged in the work of a number of public bodies, some in the role of chairman.

Sir Nigel was formally chairman of Kingfisher plc and Charterhouse Group plc and a member of the Committee on Corporate Governance (the Hampel Committee). He draws on his great breadth of experience as a board chairman and company director and the very many responsibilities he has undertaken in public life.

Linda Smith is chair of Lambeth, Southwark and Lewisham Health Authority – the second largest in the UK – and a member of the Advisory Committee on Distinction Awards for NHS consultants. She was previously chair of an NHS trust and until 1996 was Deputy Director of the Health Management Group at the City University in London. She continues as a visiting lecturer at the university, specializing in the management of change, organizational development and strategy.

In her NHS role, Linda has a special interest in the development of chairs and chief executives and the relationships between the executive and non-executive functions, as well as issues of accountability and governance in the health service. She is a founder member of the Women in Public Sector Network.

Dennis Woods is chairman and managing director of British Benzol plc, a privately owned company trading in oil on the Spot Markets in Amsterdam and London and distributing oil products to businesses and householders throughout the South of England. Ownership of the company is shared equally between the Woods family and a Dutch independent oil processing company.

British Benzol was founded as Pronto Heating Oil Ltd by Dennis Woods in 1972, as an adjunct to his parents' hardware shop. Under his leadership it has since expanded, through numerous acquisitions and organic growth, to its present size, with sales turnover of some £120 million, 150 employees and over 60 distribution tankers. The company's ethos is based on best business practice coupled with the strong family identity it still retains today.

NB. These notes relate to the circumstances prevailing when the book was first written and not to those pertaining at the time of this printing.

ABOUT THE AUTHOR

John Harper is an accomplished company director, having sat on the boards of some 30 companies in the roles of chairman, chief executive, executive director and non-executive director. He was an experienced course tutor for the Institute of Directors (IoD), where he led courses on the roles of chairman, non-executive director, company director and good board practice. He also provides personal coaching for directors and is a consultant on board matters.

Lately, John was Professional Development Director at the IoD, where he was in the forefront of establishing comprehensive training and standards of good practice for directors and boards. He was also responsible for formulating the IoD's position on corporate governance issues and establishing the professional standard relevant to Chartered Directors.

E-mail address: harper@kewgardens.demon.co.uk

Foreword

The objective of the board is to ensure the company's prosperity. To achieve it, the board must have the strategic vision to drive the business forward and to adapt it to new threats and opportunities. At the same time, the board must be mindful of its responsibility for sound corporate governance. Effective boards will have a good balance of well-chosen, competent directors. They will have clarity about their roles, accountability to shareholders, respect for the various stakeholders, and effective procedures. There will be management disciplines and there should be regularity of conduct. The board is the decision maker of the business, but it must be careful not to confuse the role of direction with that of management. It must determine the culture by which management operates and it must oversee the management of risk.

Today's boards need to be much more reactive and responsive than ever before if companies are to meet the significant challenges of a rapidly changing global marketplace. They must be sensitive to changing social, cultural and political environments. They also need to be more skilled and disciplined in using management and financial information and they must be able to harness the power of modern technology.

Above all, however, there needs to be active leadership, which can be provided by a good chairman, to ensure that the board can work as a cohesive team that is devoted to the continuing success of the enterprise. The challenge of rapid change will tax even the best led boards. It calls for the chairman to be able to exercise superior skills to ensure that the board is effective.

Successful chairmen are leaders. They succeed not just through their own knowledge and expertise, nor simply because of the strength of their personalities – they succeed because they work at the process of managing the business of the board and of identifying the methods and alliances that deliver the strategy.

In writing *Chairing the Board*, John Harper is to be congratulated in focusing his great knowledge and experience on a subject that is too often poorly understood. This book, with its practical tips and useful checklists, will continue to influence a new generation of chairmen as well as being a useful reminder to those of us who have built up some experience of the role.

Miles Templeman
Director General
Institute of Directors

Alongside his IoD role, Miles Templeman is chairman of three companies: Shepherd Neame, the Kentish family brewer; YO! Sushi, the restaurant chain; and Melrose, the buy-out specialist.

Acknowledgements

I would like to thank Michael Mander, Sir Nigel Mobbs, Linda Smith and Dennis Woods for their personal perspectives and pragmatic insights into many aspects of the complex task of chairing a board of directors. These personal views have added a very valuable and interesting dimension to the book and I have included them in the main text at the relevant places. They were obtained over some intense interviews, which were enhanced because of the care all had taken in preparing for them.

Introduction

AIMS AND SCOPE OF THE BOOK

This book is a practical handbook for those who wish to examine the potential range of their activities as chairman more comprehensively and to become more competent in the role. A useful checklist of questions is provided at the end of each chapter covering the issues raised in it. Those who chair boards of small- to medium-sized companies will probably find the book of most relevance. However, people chairing boards in the non-commercial sectors may also find many of the topics covered and the approaches adopted relevant to their situation.

The effective chairing of a board today is a proactive undertaking, and the range of activities and responsibilities that chairmen must embrace with competence and confidence is broad. Although the actual chairing of the formal meetings of the board is an important element in the overall range of responsibilities that successful chairmen must discharge, there are many other matters to be considered and mastered. Although these responsibilities essentially involve leading the board and managing its business, closer examination exposes a much broader canvas.

For example, what is the point of soldiering on with a board that is clearly not up to the job and, particularly, to meeting the challenges of the future? This question introduces the issue of board composition, which itself poses further questions, such as:

- Who should sit on the board?
- How should it be structured?
- How many directors should there be?
- What roles would be appropriate?
- How can individual directors become more effective?
- How can the board develop its effectiveness?

Then there is the matter of the board's ability to properly address all the major strategic issues that will affect the organization's viability, reputation and continuing prosperity. This in turn requires an understanding of the board's key tasks and keeping a requisite focus on tackling them. All of this demands of the chairman a sense of purpose, a vision and a set of priorities and objectives, with the skill to guide the board to focus on the relevant issues and draw out the best from each director.

Managing the board's business is perhaps centred on the planning and conduct of board meetings, where high levels of skill and competence must be developed and displayed. Surrounding this is the ability to engage all the board members and manage the relationships, requiring political skills and a nose for personal agendas. This dimension will involve acting as an effective mentor and sounding board to fellow directors and giving guidance in their personal and collective development.

I often find that there is some confusion about the true roles of the director and the board, particularly among executive directors. Many are also unclear about the full scope of the chairman's responsibilities and how their own behaviour can help or hinder the chairman's effectiveness. If this applies to members of your board, it would be sensible for you to take an active role in the process of clarification and this book should be of help to you.

All these issues and more are dealt with in this book, drawing on my work with chairmen as course leader, coach and consultant, as well as my practical experience as chairman of several company boards. These insights are augmented by illustrations from the personal observations of four experienced chairmen: Michael Mander, Sir Nigel Mobbs, Linda Smith and Dennis Woods. Their seasoned practice spans different types of organization, including large and small quoted companies, a privately owned company and a health authority in the not-for-profit sector.

ROLES AND TITLES

Although I am aware of the variety of titles used by people at the heads of boards and organizations, in this book I have used the designations of 'chairman' and 'chief executive/MD' to provide consistency. The former is used to denote a person who leads a board of directors and manages its business; the latter to denote someone with responsibility, essentially, to manage the company day-to-day, lead the employees and deliver the operating performance of the company. The use of the designation 'chief executive/MD' in this book reflects the fact that the titles 'chief executive' and 'managing director' are both in common use by people doing the job in the UK, as is the US title CEO (chief executive officer). So the designation is merely used to identify the role played, whichever title might actually be used in practice.

It may be worthwhile to reflect for a moment on what the title of the board's leader might properly be today. I don't wish to get into the shifting sands of perceived political correctness here, recognizing that the terms 'chairperson' or 'chair' are *de rigueur* in many organizations. On the other hand, I appreciate that these terms are derided or frowned upon by others. I therefore use the traditional epithet 'chairman' in this book simply to identify a role to be played, without connotations of gender. Although the titles 'executive chairman' or 'non-executive chairman' are sometimes used, I don't find them particularly appropriate. The title 'executive chairman' usually denotes that the holder is fulfilling the dual roles of both chairman and chief executive/MD, in which case the proper title 'chairman and chief executive' makes that fact clear. There seems little point in calling oneself 'non-executive chairman' when everyone knows that the role of chairman of the board does not involve managing the company in any way. So the straightforward title of 'chairman' seems to be the sensible one to use, bearing in mind that one is chairman of the board, not chairman of the company.

Many chairmen also fulfil the role of chief executive/MD of the company, although some are not entirely clear as to what is really required of them in these quite distinct roles. A number regard the role of chairman as the more prestigious but apply most of their energy and time to the other role. Their fellow directors are often confused as to which role is which and what their proper relationship with the leader should be in each situation. Where that is the case, I hope this book will help in clarifying matters.

FOCUS ON SUCCESSFUL DIRECTION

The sheer rate of change occurring in all quarters of our environment – commercial, political, technological, economic, social – puts increased pressure on all organizations to adapt, change, refocus, develop, improve, succeed – or die. In this environment, many of the old paradigms no longer apply, or must be considered in a changing context. The differentiation between day-to-day management, leadership and direction may be less clear, but the need to look ahead, change and adapt is more necessary, more important and often more pressing than ever before. The imperatives of directing, providing leadership, innovating and protecting, while taking necessary risks, are more important than ever in these circumstances. Differentiating direction from day-to-day management while recognizing the essential dynamic interchange that is necessary to perform well continuously in the shifting sands of today's strategic environment is as vital as ever.

These features require that the professionalism, competence and effectiveness of the group of people who make the key decisions about where the organization is heading, how it will get there and what risks it should take – the board of directors – must be of a very high order. It is the chairman of the board who must accept the responsibility for ensuring that the board delivers this high level of effectiveness. This has to be the real focus of the modern chairman and is what this book is really all about – your success, your board's success and the continuing prosperity of the organization it serves.

1

The board's proper role

It may come as a surprise to you, but many of the boards of directors that I encounter today are not really sure what their proper function is. There is often confusion concerning which are the really important issues for the board to consider and what should be left for others to decide. Executive directors are frequently unsure of what is expected of them in the boardroom. Management matters are intermingled with board matters. Governance is a topic that habitually induces an attitude of indifference in many directors.

For all these reasons I would ask you to start by reading this first chapter as both a refresher and a stimulus, then see to it that all the members of your board are clear in their understanding of these matters. You can then go forward with more confidence to improve both your chairmanship and the effectiveness of your board.

THE BOARD'S PURPOSE

Directors' responsibilities

Do all the directors on your board have a clear appreciation of what their duties are and what the board is there for? Is it clear to them that it is a legal requirement that every incorporated company must have directors or at least a director? Often, the Articles of Association will stipulate the minimum and/or maximum number of directors that the company shall have. Are they familiar with the Articles of the company that they serve? Similar mandates usually apply where directors are appointed to the governing bodies of other types of organization that are not incorporated as companies but which operate in similar ways.

The directors have collective responsibility in law as a board of directors for the affairs of the organization to which they have been appointed. All directors on a board share their legal responsibilities equally, whether they are executive or non-executive directors and regardless of any particular duties they may have as employees or shareholdings they may possess. They also share collective responsibility for how the company is managed and for how the company (and therefore its staff) behaves. Accordingly, they must see that the company obeys the law and any regulations that circumscribe its activities.

In the case of a company, the board has full and ultimate responsibility for the wellbeing of the company, its affairs, its actions and those of its employees. The shareholders effectively put their company in the board's trust, usually giving considerable power to the directors. So on this level, the directors act as stewards of the company on behalf of the shareholders, and are legally responsible. Directors owe fiduciary duties to the company, which means that they are required to act in good faith in its best interests, not misapply their powers, nor create a conflict between their duties to the company and their personal interests or duties to third parties. (This is an over-simplification of a complex subject. All directors should fully acquaint themselves with their legal duties and liabilities. Appendix 1 at the back of this book gives a useful overview. It is an excerpt from *Standards for the Board* (2001), published by the Institute of Directors and Kogan Page. Useful reference books dealing with the subject are: Gore-Browne *et al*, *Gore-Browne on Companies;* Tolley's *Company Law Handbook;* and Sinclair *et al*, *Company Directors: Law and Liability.*)

By taking responsibility for the company's wellbeing, the board must ensure that the company survives and prospers. (Here, I am ignoring those few occasions when a company is being wound up or operated for a finite short-term purpose, or is dormant.) In this respect, the directors of an incorporated company and those acting as a board of an organization that is not incorporated have a similar role. The board must therefore shape the destiny of the organization, ensure its ongoing financial performance and safeguard its interests and reputation. These responsibilities are clearly separate from any that individual directors may have as managers or as shareholders in the company.

These responsibilities imply that the over-arching purpose of the board is to *ensure the company's continuing prosperity.* Everything it does should be conducted with this purpose in mind, requiring a generally forward-looking, longer-term perspective. However, in deciding what may be in the best interest of the company and its continuing prosperity, the board must consider the company's interaction with other parties. In this context the interests of the shareholders are clearly pertinent, as are those of employees, customers and suppliers. It is for the board to consider the extent to which it is appropriate to take into account the interests or influences of these and other parties.

It is essential that all the directors of an organization understand these matters and are clear as to what they must do to ensure that the company's prosperity is assured. As chairman, you should undertake to make sure that this universal clarity exists, as a prerequisite to better board performance. In doing so, you will almost certainly discover some confusion and ignorance.

The board's complex role

Although the board is responsible for the good management of the organization, it must clearly delegate this function to the management. This is because the board of directors is fundamentally a decision making body; it has neither the time nor the resources itself to do much else. Remember that all the information that the board considers, all the questions that are asked and all the discussions that take place at board meetings should have only two outcomes. One, the most fundamental, is to *make decisions,* good ones for the most part, and the other is to *learn.*

Your main focus as chairman is to ensure that the board concentrates its energy and wisdom on the appropriate matters requiring decisions and is competent to come to suitable conclusions. The management should be given the authority to implement those decisions of the board, usually through the chief executive/MD. The board should pass a resolution that clearly gives such authority.

The learning process requires an honest and objective review of the board's wrong and poor decisions, so that lessons can be learnt from them. Periodic reviews of the board's processes, how directors behave and the way information is presented and considered are all useful ways of improving the board's effectiveness by learning. Directors will also learn from one another and from your mentoring activity, as well as from the actions of others. These matters will be addressed in later chapters.

The board must make judgements on a whole range of issues that might affect the organization. These judgements will involve evaluating various pieces of information, considering the relevance of each and putting them in context. The relevant information and other criteria must then be weighed carefully before a decision is made. These decisions and the perceptions that underpin them should call upon the collective opinions, knowledge, attitudes and experience of the board members. However, the advantages of such a collective perspective can only be achieved if the chairman makes sure that the full potential of each director is realized. Clearly, if the directors are ill equipped to address the complexity and scope of the issues that face them, or if they are not able to come together effectively, then something must be done. This will require a review of the board's constitution, processes and effectiveness, with consequent action. These are all matters for the chairman to tackle and will be dealt with later in this book. If the shortcomings are exacerbated by poor chairmanship, perhaps this book will be of help.

The complexity of business and society today and the rapidity and breadth of change that is taking place call for more competent and effective boards of directors than ever before. Their collective wisdom and competence must often deal with matters of great complexity that are sometimes apparently contradictory. They must display a sense of responsibility at all times and yet be prepared to take risks and be somewhat detached from day-to-day business. They should often think abstractly, sometimes with their heads in the clouds, and yet be pragmatic and down-to-earth.

For most companies it is very unlikely that any individual, however knowledgeable and intelligent, could accommodate the sheer scope of this complexity and the range and subtlety of the issues that are germane to these many contradictions. This is the primary reason why a group of directors – a board – is necessary for a modern company. Several heads are better than one in this case, as long as the directors have the diversity and depth of experience and knowledge the situation demands, together with the attributes and skills needed to be an effective team. The leadership of the board by the chairman is another important ingredient for board effectiveness.

Probably your most challenging tasks as chairman are to create and lead a board that is truly capable of addressing these diversities and making well-balanced judgements when faced with conflicting challenges. We will address these issues in subsequent chapters.

Some of these seemingly contradictory demands that boards face are referred to in *Standards for the Board* (Institute of Directors, 2001) in the following way:

- The board must simultaneously be entrepreneurial and drive the business forward while keeping it under prudent control.
- The board is required to be sufficiently knowledgeable about the workings of the company to be answerable for its actions, yet to be able to stand back from the day-to-day management of the company and retain an objective, long-term view.
- The board must be sensitive to the pressures of short-term issues and yet be informed about broader, long-term trends.
- The board must be knowledgeable about 'local' issues and yet be aware of potential or actual non-local, increasingly international, competitive and other influences.
- The board is expected to be focused upon the commercial needs of its business while acting responsibly towards its employees, business partners and society as a whole.

A confusion of roles often arises when all or some of the directors are also significant shareholders in the company. Under such circumstances it is all too easy for board meetings to also become shareholders' meetings on occasion, with a consequent confusion of objectives. It is better that you take the initiative to defer shareholder issues for separate consideration, by the shareholders, at another meeting with its own agenda. If you are a chairman with a major shareholding, or represent the holding company of a subsidiary, it is important to avoid dominating the board. Remember that the directors have a collective legal responsibility to act in the best interests of the company at all times, within regulatory, legal and ethical constraints. Their judgements in this regard will be conditioned by what the shareholders as a whole might expect, but they are required to take other matters into account as well. Each director should have equal weighting in the board's decision making process, unaffected by any shareholding they may or may not have. As chairman of the board you should aim at helping the board to realize its overall purpose and to discharge its responsibilities. You should also guard against any tendency you may have to perhaps gratify your personal wishes.

Leadership

There is often some confusion around the issue of leadership as far as the board of directors is concerned. Such confusion is often compounded when one person is both the chairman and the chief executive/MD. The matter is complicated because there are really three separate leadership roles to be undertaken.

One leadership role is met by the board, in that the board of directors has its part to play in providing the company with leadership in a general sense. Here we are concerned with the board determining such matters as the ethos of the company, its values, standards of behaviour, pace, attitude to risk and change and providing a sense of direction. It must also choose a chief executive/MD who will personify those factors when acting in the day-to-day role of leading the employees of the company. This role of senior manager as leader is probably the one that is most readily recognized and understood by most people. The chairman has the quite separate but important role of leading the board and managing its business.

So, in different ways, leadership is displayed by the board, the chief executive/MD and the chairman. All the parties concerned must play their part in avoiding confusion by keeping these three leadership roles distinct. In particular, as the chairman, you should refrain from appearing to act as the leader of the employees from time to time and leave that job unequivocally to the chief executive/MD. If you are both chairman and chief executive/MD, be careful to separate your two personal leadership roles so that those around you are clear as to what role you are playing in every circumstance. This is particularly important when conducting board meetings or management meetings. Remember that you are chairman of the board, not chairman of the company.

Experienced chairmen expressed the following views on the topics covered in this section

Sir Nigel Mobbs

I do think that there is a very distinct difference in purpose between a board's role and the role of management. The former role is to direct a business and to oversee the interests of the shareholders, while the latter is actually to take the strategies agreed by the board and implement them. In this, the chairman's role is to provide leadership to the board and to ensure that the disciplines appropriate to the board are in place and to distinguish between the board's role and that of management. The chief executive / MD will provide leadership to the management. At the end of it, the chairman has the responsibility to see that the chief executive / MD carries out what the board expects. Although the board has the job of doing that in concept, it is really for the chairman to be the persona of the board in terms of the interface with the chief executive / MD on a personal basis. Clearly, if this breaks down, the board may have to act on a collective basis, but the majority of the dialogue between the chief executive / MD and the board will be with the chairman.

Applying the corporate governance 'sets of rules' can be too restrictive of good corporate leadership and even a positive handicap to it, in that playing the role of leader well can become more difficult.

Linda Smith

It is a struggle to keep the issue of its proper role in front of the board. I feel that if I take my eye off the ball it starts to drift toward the old way of doing things. That's where people in the organization feel that they work on something which is a particular policy, requiring planning and consultation, and then present it to the board, where comments and questions are made at the edge that don't really have too much of an impact on what is presented. I've tried to steer the board away from that approach. When we do have important strategic issues to consider, they come to the board with some labels on them, identifying what the writer thinks they want from the board and what the board can add. If this is done sufficiently early in the process, they can get an overall view of where the board wants it to go, then they can go away and the detail gets built into it.

DIRECTING, NOT MANAGING

The board is responsible for directing the company and is the principal agent of risk taking. This means focusing on providing overall leadership, judgement and enterprise and on making those decisions that are *central* to protecting and enhancing the interests of the company over time. This cannot be done if the board is bogged down with day-to-day matters that are the proper concern of executive management. It is a prime responsibility of the chairman to maintain this focus.

Many chairmen, particularly where the directors are all or mostly executive, have some difficulty getting their board to stay focused on matters of direction. Too often, they find board meetings becoming hybrids, with more detailed management matters evolving from legitimate agenda items or merely creeping into the meeting's business unannounced. Does this sound familiar? If so, there are a number of practical remedies that I can suggest.

A good starting point is to consider how well each of your executive directors really understands what is required of them as a director:

- Are they quite clear about the responsibilities and purpose of a board of directors?
- Do they have a clear understanding of how they should behave as a director and what duties they have in law?
- Have they seen the Memorandum and Articles of Association of the company they are directors of and do they know what those documents are for?

- Are they familiar with the various tasks that a board should be competent in addressing and how they can add to that competence?
- Can they effectively separate their roles as directors from their executive management roles?

If the answer to all or any of these questions is either 'no' or 'not adequately', there are things you can do that will help.

You can insist that the executive directors put the necessary time aside to remedy their deficiencies through reading and attending suitable courses. (The courses provided by the Institute of Directors (IoD) are ideal for this purpose.) This learning process can then be augmented by means of mentoring sessions with you. Try starting with an explanation of what you need to achieve in your role as chairman and how they can play their part in helping you to succeed. After all, it is unlikely that many of them have given much thought to what is entailed in fulfilling the chairman's role successfully. In doing so, be sure to ask them to play their part in keeping matters that should be dealt with at management meetings out of discussions at board meetings. If they are subsequently guilty of this bad habit, you can remind them again during your mentoring sessions with them.

Then consider their job descriptions. All executive directors should have a written statement of what their responsibilities are, which I find almost invariably cover only what is expected of them as an executive. If this is the case with your directors, don't be too surprised if they focus their energies on what is written in their job descriptions and regard their directing roles as incidental to what they could legitimately feel to be their paramount functions. You can change this state of affairs by either adding a list of their responsibilities as directors to the present documents, preferably at the top, or creating separate statements of their responsibilities as directors. The latter approach is probably preferable because it reinforces the fact that they have two quite separate and important roles to fulfil.

You can also encourage your directors to see directorship as a discrete profession. This will require them to obtain and successfully apply a particular range of knowledge and to conduct themselves in a pertinently professional manner. The IoD has established the criteria to be met by those who become Chartered Directors, which is the professional standard. You may wish to encourage directors on your board to attain that distinction.

One of the important criteria that the IoD has laid down for Chartered Directors is that they must undertake to adhere to a Code of Professional Conduct for directors. This Code has 12 Articles, with which any and all directors could and perhaps should comply. By doing so they would demonstrate their commitment to professionalism and probity. If you could induce your fellow directors to undertake such a commitment, you would help them to understand and delineate more fully their director role. At the same time, it would help greatly to enhance the professional focus and behaviour of the whole board. The captions of the 12 articles are reproduced below. They stipulate that a director shall:

1. Exercise leadership, enterprise and judgement in directing the company so as to achieve its continuing prosperity and act in the best interests of the company as a whole.
2. Follow the standards of good practice set out in the Institute's 'Good Practice for Directors – Standards for the Board' and act accordingly and diligently.
3. Serve the legitimate interests of the company's shareholders.
4. Exercise responsibilities to employees, customers, suppliers and other relevant stakeholders, including the wider community.
5. Comply with relevant laws, regulations and codes of practice, refrain from anti-competitive practices, and honour obligations and commitments.
6. At all times have a duty to respect the truth and act honestly in business dealings and in the exercise of all responsibilities as a director.
7. Avoid conflict between personal interests, or interests of any associated company or person, and his or her duties to the company.
8. Not make improper use of information acquired as a director or disclose, or allow to be disclosed, information confidential to the company.

9. Not recklessly or maliciously injure the professional reputation of another director and not engage in any practice detrimental to the reputation and interests of the profession of director.

10. Ensure that he or she keeps abreast of current good practice in directing.

11. Set high personal standards by keeping aware of and adhering to this Code, both in the spirit and in the letter, and promoting it to other directors.

12. Apply the principles of this Code appropriately when acting as a director of a non-commercial organization.

Most appointments as executive director will have been made principally on the strength of success as a manager or senior specialist. Many such directors will regard their appointment to the role of director merely as a further endorsement of that success in the operational field, rather than the taking on of a completely separate, additional mantle. Their management role requires them to achieve results in the domain for which they have responsibility and to 'get things done'. In contrast, their director role requires an essentially thoughtful, reflective approach of 'thinking things through' in conjunction with their board colleagues. They must take action to create sufficient time to think and act as directors. This means delegating more of their management role to others and resisting getting involved in things that interest them and the solution to every crisis. They should also always see their managerial actions in the context of the objectives and strategies that have been agreed by the board. Your wise counsel will undoubtedly assist your executive directors to understand properly what their director appointment requires of them and how to fulfil that role competently.

One effective way to differentiate the board's role from that of the management is to have the board discuss and agree those topics that are in its proper domain. Such matters are sometimes referred to as *the board's reserved powers* and should be listed. Each director should have a copy. These will be primarily those essential topics that will shape and determine the destiny of the organization, its ethos, achievements, structure, reputation, wellbeing and posture within the law. They will also include some statutory matters, authority levels, etc. Any other matters should normally be off the board's agenda and left for management to decide upon. This will help you to maintain a clearly understood division between the board's role and that of management and help the executive directors on the board to play their two separate roles more effectively. We will return to this matter in more detail in Chapter 3.

Having some non-executive directors on the board provides many advantages and is vital for obtaining proper balance and effectiveness. One advantage is that their presence at board meetings mandates that management matters are dealt with elsewhere and any capable non-executive director would reinforce this. We shall look at board composition in Chapter 5.

Be very careful when you are drawing up agendas for board meetings. Make sure that all items are strictly board matters and that reports from management do not invite the board to solve management problems. Make a set of rules of behaviour for the conduct of board meetings that all directors should subscribe to. Then insist that everyone adhere to the rules. We will address these matters more comprehensively in Chapter 6.

If you are both chairman and chief executive/MD, make sure that you keep both roles clearly separate. At board meetings and at management meetings, don't switch from one role to the other, or the executive directors may become confused as to which role you are playing and which meeting they are really attending. Convene board meetings on different days to the monthly management meetings to help clearly differentiate the two events. Also consider having board meetings less frequently than management meetings and conducting board meetings with rather more formality than other meetings.

Experienced chairmen expressed the following views on some of the topics covered in this section

Sir Nigel Mobbs

There are difficulties in getting some executive directors to act and think as directors, rather than as managers all the time. One problem is that senior managers often feel that they should become directors by right. Yet, some are not entirely suited to the role because they aren't able to take the broad view required by directors. It is often an onerous task to persuade them to take a company perspective and to stop still seeing themselves only as the head of a particular function or professional group within the company. One obvious way to help overcome the difficulty is to choose appointees for the right reasons. Then, particularly when promoting from within the company, get them to take time off to attend suitable courses and conferences to make them think about it – it helps to change the mindset. It is also a good idea for the chairman to give them both a major and a minor role in relation to the board so that they are taken out of the confines of their major executive responsibility. This helps them to see the bigger picture too by providing another focus.

Dennis Woods

Many directors find it difficult to differentiate between being a director and being a manager, but I never have. My parents were also part of the business initially and, as we all lived together, matters were discussed informally and we later referred to these agreements as business decisions. However, right from the start I also held proper, formal board meetings that made things move forward. We formally made decisions, minuted them and, when we next met, reviewed those situations and moved on. I have always differentiated between being a director, being a manager and being an owner of the company. My executive director colleagues do sometimes struggle with this differentiation. Often I have to point out to them that a matter is not a departmental issue, where as a manager they could be fighting their corner, but something on which we must make a decision that is right for the company as a whole.

I keep a good relationship with each of the directors and sit down with them individually at times. I find it helps all of us to take an opportunity to chat it through over a cup of coffee on a very low-key basis – just keep chipping away at it. Executive directors can learn about the essential responsibilities and duties of directors by attending courses on the subject. Then we can reinforce what has been learnt and help put it in context. I also find that conducting board meetings with due formality, with well-structured agendas and minutes and formal reviews, helps keep board responsibilities separate and distinct from day-to-day management jobs.

Linda Smith

I think there has been a lack of clarity around the role of the board and therefore a lot of things have flowed from that. As you know, boards in the NHS are made up of executive and non-executive directors. I do try to form a board that is a corporate board with corporate responsibility – I am trying to get executive directors to make a distinction between their managerial role and their board role, which is sometimes not easy. My approach to it has been that if the board as a whole has been playing its proper role it is much easier for non-executive and executive directors to have a proper relationship and to be carrying out their own individual roles within that.

THE BOARD'S KEY TASKS

The tasks that the board should address are essentially those that will determine the ongoing prosperity of the company – which is the overriding purpose of the board. These tasks fall into two key areas, which I have labelled the 'conditioning' tasks and the 'enterprise' tasks. The *conditioning* area is largely about the company's aspirations, values and its interface with other parties. The *enterprise* area is concerned with the specific direction in which the company will develop. The first task area will clearly condition the other.

The IoD, in its publication *Standards for the Board*, has categorized these tasks under four main headings. What I have called the 'conditioning' tasks are described as *Establishing vision, mission and values* and *Exercising accountability to shareholders and being responsible to relevant stakeholders.* The 'enterprise' tasks are categorized as *Setting strategy and structure* and *Delegating to management.* I recommend that you and your board colleagues become familiar with these standards. In them you will find that the four key tasks of the board are each sub-divided into four more discrete tasks, each with a set of questions that might be asked in relation to their execution. There is also a useful summary of the legal duties and liabilities of company directors, a section on board effectiveness and one on directors' knowledge and skills.

The 'conditioning' tasks will require the board to agree the sort of organization the company should be in the future, how it will be perceived and how third parties are to be treated. This process can start with posing the simple questions: What is or will be the reason for this company's existence? What is or will be its purpose? What will be special about our company that it can continue to prosper and stay relevant in the future? Whatever statement of the company's purpose transpires from these deliberations, it is vital that all the people who work in the organization can align their thoughts and efforts towards its realization. Unless this happens it is likely to remain a dream. Perhaps that is why I prefer to use the term 'purpose' rather than 'vision'. However, some companies have a separate but related statement of a desired future state that the company will ideally attain, called a 'vision statement'. For many, purpose and vision in this context have similar meanings; that is, something to aspire to, described in a statement of what the company ideally wants to achieve. The matter of how to realize that state is often written as a set of goals or 'mission' for the organization to attain.

Not surprisingly perhaps, most of your board's time will be taken up with carrying out the 'enterprise' tasks. That is not because they are more important than the 'conditioning' tasks; indeed, if you don't know where you are going and why, one could argue that further activity is at best lacking in real purpose. Rather, it is that once the organization's future purpose and ethos have been agreed, together with the policies that support them, they will probably be set for a long period. The board's main concern in this area will then be to see that they are being appropriately endorsed by staff in the company and understood by relevant people outside it.

The 'enterprise' tasks of the board can be broadly considered as deciding how the company will achieve the goals to attain its declared purpose in the light of its circumstances and then making sure that they are carried through effectively. Some of these decisions will relate to the provision of resources and the formation of strategic alliances. The primary focus should be strategic, usually involving competition, risk and a constant shift in the environment in which the company operates.

Although the board must delegate the day-to-day management of the company to the chief executive/MD, it is still responsible for the way in which the company is managed. The board can delegate authority but it cannot delegate its ultimate responsibility for the actions of all the employees.

We will look into how the board should properly address these tasks in subsequent chapters of this book. At this juncture it is sufficient to make the point that every chairman should ensure that the board addresses the board's tasks comprehensively and effectively.

> An experienced chairman expressed the following views on some of the topics covered in this section
>
> *Linda Smith*
>
> We have a big performance management role, both in regard to our own strategic direction and those laid down by government. The latter are more and more a list of things that we must do if we are to get the extra finance we need – this is part of our accountability upwards. Government has a right to lay down these requirements. After all, they are elected and we are not, we are appointed. They feel they have a mandate to reflect public concerns and priorities and they do control the public purse.

GOVERNANCE

The board is exclusively responsible for the governance of the company, which can be defined as 'the accomplishment, manner or system of directing and controlling the affairs, policies, functions and actions of an organization'. It should therefore focus on giving leadership, directing the organization's affairs and overseeing what is being done.

The practice of good corporate governance is therefore an essential concern for all boards of directors. Although it is of particular relevance to directors of listed companies, it has also become a matter of increasing interest and pertinence to boards of other companies and corporate bodies in recent years – a trend that is set to continue. This is why competent chairmen should become familiar with the issues and trends in corporate governance practice and consider which aspects might be applicable to the boards of their organizations and when. The topic is referred to in more depth in Appendix 2.

There has been much discussion on the subject of corporate governance in relation to companies that are listed on the London Stock Exchange. This has culminated in the requirement for such companies to provide an annual statement of their compliance with the *Combined Code on Corporate Governance* (2003), or reasons for non-compliance. There is an overview of the *Code* in Appendix 2, including a transcript of the guidance given on the role of the chairman; here is a summary:

> *The chairman is pivotal in creating the conditions for overall board and individual director effectiveness, both inside and outside the boardroom. Specifically, it is the responsibility of the chairman to:*
>
> - *Run the board and set its agenda. Agendas should take full account of the issues and the concerns of all board members, be forward looking and concentrate on strategic matters.*
> - *Ensure that the members of the board receive accurate, timely and clear information.*
> - *Ensure effective communication with shareholders.*
> - *Manage the board to ensure that sufficient time is allowed for discussion of complex or contentious issues.*
> - *Take the lead in providing a properly constructed induction programme for new directors.*
> - *Take the lead in identifying and meeting the development needs of individual directors and addressing the development needs of the board as a whole with a view to enhancing its overall effectiveness as a team.*
> - *Ensure that the performance of individuals and of the board as a whole and its committees is evaluated at least once a year.*
> - *Encourage active engagement by all the members of the board.*

Even with organizations that do not operate under the constraints that apply to listed companies, there is much to be said for having a balance of power and authority at the top, where it is practicable.

This is particularly true for organizations operating in the public and not-for-profit sectors, where the transparency of accountability and issues of probity are paramount concerns. Such balance is best achieved by having separate chairman and chief executive/MD and a group of competent, strong-minded non-executive directors. We will consider board balance including non-executive directors in chapter 5 and the relationship between the chairman and the chief executive/MD in chapter 7.

DECISION MAKING

The board of directors is essentially a decision making body – it has neither the time nor the resources to do much else. Bearing this in mind, it is clear that your most important objective as chairman is to try to ensure that your board makes the best possible decisions. Here we are concerned with those important decisions that will ensure the ongoing prosperity, viability, relevance and good reputation of the organization. It is therefore essential that you and your board colleagues have an understanding of the decision making process and what can be done to provide the best chance of producing good decisions.

Decision making is quite a complex subject in itself, requiring a deep understanding to do it true justice. Nevertheless, it is appropriate to reflect on some of the essentials here, in the context of the board of directors.

A decision is usually regarded as a commitment to a course of action, despite the fact that choosing to do nothing is as much a decision as any other. The board must use its collective experience, wisdom, creativity and judgement to seek and evaluate the views and information it requires, and then to decide. Each decision will be expected to be appropriate for a certain length of time. Although all or most of the board's decisions will have longer-term implications and might be expected to be relevant for some time, it is likely that changing circumstances will require many to be re-evaluated. This makes many of them provisional by nature, even though they may be essentially long term. Most of the decisions made by a board of directors will have implications that are manifested elsewhere. This is because the board delegates authority for others to implement its decisions.

Directors must use their brains – they are paid to think. A well-informed decision will be arrived at by a process of copious thinking, where all options have been considered and where every implication has been fully understood. This implies that the quality of the thinking involved in the process must be of a very high order if sound, first-rate decisions are to be made. Such good quality thinking recognizes that the information available in relation to the decision can never be complete and comprehensive. In practical terms, this implies that the decisions that boards have to make will involve evaluating the relevance of what information is and might be available, deciding what can be made available and making judgements in that light.

The act of deciding will require the board to choose from alternatives. Part of the thinking process is to think out those alternatives – looking for different possible outcomes from which to make a choice. The weighing of information and using imagination to fill the gaps involves the use of perceptual thinking – the subsequent choices with judgmental thinking. In his book *How to be a Better Decision Maker,* Barker (1997) describes these two stages where, 'In the first stage, we look at reality and name what we see. We find a way of talking about it; we turn reality into a language. In the second, we make sense of reality by manipulating the language.'

The improvement of the board's decision making requires attention to both these types of thinking, particularly perceptual thinking. Rational judgements applied to poorly perceived alternatives will inevitably produce poor results. If the perception of a situation is narrow and restricted, the board's ability to decide what to do will be severely limited, regardless of how good the directors may be in using judgmental thinking. It is therefore vital that the board develops the ability to broaden its perception in order that it creates the necessary alternatives from which to choose. Such thinking therefore requires the predicting of what might pertain, the understanding of the situation, the in-depth evaluation of probabilities and the balancing of possible risk and reward. It involves making assumptions and takes into account both what might happen and what might go wrong. However, the board can never know everything about the context of the decisions it must make, and in any case circumstances may change in the course of time. Neither can the board be certain of the consequences of implementing those decisions, since many of the consequences may not be immediately apparent.

Even though the board's decisions will be affected by the directors' collective experience of being involved in previous decisions, it is constraining to rely solely on such past experience. Most of these decisions will be set in a future context, which will inevitably be somewhat different from the past and the present. This is why the board's thinking must go beyond the limits of past experience. It is also why the board's experience must often be augmented by the views, concepts and insights of others.

A decision is only successful in its implementation with the commitment, enthusiasm and cooperation of those who must bring it into effect. That is why most board decisions must not be made in isolation and why the views and commitment of the executive directors, who will be involved in their implementation, are so important.

> An experienced chairman expresses the following views on some of the topics covered in this section
>
> *Linda Smith*
>
> You get into difficulties when the board is not clear about its role and where it is 'rubber stamping' – this is when you have executive directors coming to a board meeting and presenting papers, with non-executive directors asking questions and then things going through 'on the nod'. I think that is one of the risks that one can get into because the non-executive directors may make the assumption that the executives know best because they are doing it every day, so how can we possibly challenge. Indeed, it is sometimes difficult to have the proper degree of challenge, which is one of the roles of the non-executive director – to scrutinize, if you like, and to be a sounding board and challenge to the operational, managerial work. They can't do that sometimes if they feel that they have to know as much about it as the executive directors, which they will never do. I think that, if boards are playing their proper role, it is then much easier to function.

CHAPTER CHECKLIST

Here are some questions you might ask yourself in connection with the matters covered in this chapter before you plan any consequent action:

- Are all directors on your board clear about their legal duties and responsibilities?
- Have they read and understood the Memorandum and Articles of Association?
- Do they know what the key purpose of the board is?
- Are they clear what they must do to assure that the purpose is achieved?
- Do they realize that the board is essentially there to *make decisions* that are central to protecting and enhancing the interests of the company and its shareholders over time?
- ... and that other matters should be decided by the management team?
- Does your company's management have a clear mandate to do this?
- Does your board learn from what it does, how it functions and from what others do?
- Do you draw on the full range of opinions, attitudes, knowledge and experience potentially available from your directors?
- ... and are these adequate to address the complexity and diversity of issues likely to face your board?
- If significant shareholders are also directors, do matters that are strictly for shareholders sometimes make their way onto the board's business?
- Are you frequently guilty of dominating the board because of the power you hold?
- ... or of gratifying your personal wishes?
- Do you refrain from appearing to act as leader of the staff at all times (unless you are also the chief executive/MD)?
- If you are chairman and chief executive/MD, are you careful always to separate your two leadership roles so that everyone always knows which role you are playing?
- ... and will you consider dividing these responsibilities between two people at the appropriate time?

- Do your board meetings focus exclusively on matters of direction or do they frequently become involved with issues that are more properly dealt with at management meetings?
- Are your board meetings and executive management meetings clearly differentiated?
- Do the executive directors understand how their role as director differs from their role as executive manager?
- ... and are they familiar with a Professional Code which will encourage them to see their directorship as a discrete profession?
- Is it apparent to them that their director role requires that they 'think things through', whereas their management role is focused on 'getting things done'?
- Do you act as a mentor or coach for your directors to help them become more knowledgeable, competent and effective as directors?
- Is this process augmented by their attendance on courses and by relevant reading?
- Do they know how they can help you to be a more effective chairman?
- Are the executive directors each equipped with a written list of their responsibilities as directors, distinct from their management responsibilities?
- Does your board have a list of those powers reserved to itself?
- ... and is the chief executive/MD empowered to decide on a list of subordinate matters?
- Does your board understand its 'conditioning' tasks and is it capable of addressing them effectively?
- Is your board familiar with its 'enterprise' tasks and can it meet them comprehensively?
- Are your directors familiar with those corporate governance issues that might affect your board?
- Are you and your board colleagues fully aware of how the decision making process can work to provide the best opportunity for good decisions to be made?
- ... requiring high quality perceptual and judgmental thinking?

2

Focusing on strategic issues

ANTICIPATING THE FUTURE

It can be argued that the future is like a strange country where nobody has been before – an unknown place. It is very difficult to make decisions with any degree of certainty about the unknown future. Yet, unless your organization is currently facing a question of its imminent demise, the most important concern of the board has to be the organization's future. What has happened has already happened and the company is where it is – only future prosperity really matters. This requires the board to form some idea of what the company will be like in the future and how it will perform in its future environment. And yet, too many boards spend too much of their time looking in the rear view mirror instead of looking ahead and trying to anticipate what is around the next bend and how to negotiate it.

A company has the potential to last forever, since its shareholders can pass on their shares to others and the board of directors will change over time. Isn't it ironic, therefore, that few companies last longer than a human life span? Even those that survive their early years without becoming financially non-viable frequently run out of steam and are acquired by another company and become integrated into its existing activities. Either way, the company ceases to exist as an independent organization under the direction of its board, with the original potential of seeing the world as its oyster and having the opportunity to make its own pearls.

A board that is constituted of people who are good 'doers', who find it difficult or impossible to contemplate the somewhat imponderable issues concerning the future and to think creatively will almost always be doomed to compromise the company's potential. This is one reason why perhaps the most important responsibility of a chairman is to ensure that the board contains a balance of people who are able to properly address the issues that will give the company a good chance of surviving, prospering and realizing its full potential.

From time to time, the board must address such searching questions as:

- 'What must we do to ensure that the company is relevant in the future?'
- 'What will the company's future purpose be?'
- 'How will we sustain our position in the changing business environment that lies ahead?'
- 'What are these changes likely to be and what opportunities and threats might they pose?'
- 'How could we exploit those opportunities by moving into new areas on a sufficient scale?'
- 'What resources will we need and should we develop them or acquire them?'

It is generally accepted good practice today for boards to consider these and related questions at a special meeting, separate from the normal board meetings and often held at a different location. It sometimes helps to have an external facilitator to at least begin the process of thinking through these issues, sometimes with the inclusion of individuals from within the company below board level. The process of drawing conclusions and making the final decisions can then be carried out by the board itself, under the chairman's guidance. Only when the board has a clear vision of where it wants the organization to be in the future – what kind of organization, engaged in what, how, where, what size, etc – can appropriate strategies be thought through, to determine how that vision might be fulfilled.

In thinking these matters through, the board must consider the likely changes in the many dimensions of the environment in which the company will operate. This might be done by using the well-known PEST analysis, where the likely Political, Economic, Social and Technological changes are taken into account. To this should be added consideration of geographic, market, supplier, shareholder and stakeholder issues. The board should also contemplate what current and potential competitors might do and the likely impact of future mergers and acquisitions in the industry sectors concerned.

Such a vision for the future organization should be a somewhat ideal concept, yet be clear enough to give a sense of purpose to everyone in the organization. Underpinning the vision will be the values and ethics that the organization will uphold and which form the bedrock of its corporate culture. That culture may need to change over time to ensure that the company accommodates the changes necessary for it to prosper in tomorrow's world. From this entire process will come a number of goals for the company, strategies to achieve those goals and perhaps some new or modified policies.

The word 'vision' implies a rather vague notion for some directors, quite unrelated to the tough business world in which they are engaged. They would probably agree, however, that it is good practice for people to have a sense of purpose and goals to aim at and might find it acceptable to see the creation of a 'vision' as a means of achieving them. Colin Sworder (1995) relates a corporate vision to common beliefs a board can develop, about the possibilities for their business, their markets, their employees and themselves. The following is from his contribution in *Developing Strategic Thought:*

> *Corporate visions have become the subject of debate in recent years. Many world-class and successful organizations have one. Other organizations eschew them, regarding them as hype or worse. There is some research which affirms that individuals and groups who have clear visions invariably achieve them. There is a basic premise that human beings are drawn towards and become like the dominant images we hold in our minds.*

> *So who needs a 'vision'? What is a vision anyway? Well, every human being has a vision and many of the best 'envisioners' are under 10 years old. 'It's easy for them, they don't have to meet performance targets' is a common response. That's true. It also explains why many people over the age of 10 can find it quite difficult. What restricts our thinking is the certain knowledge or belief that some things are achievable and others not. This applies to us as individuals, groups, teams and nations. It is these beliefs which can keep us alive, or not, as Icarus discovered too late. We develop our beliefs, in the main, over fairly lengthy periods of time and many factors play a part in their formation. A board can develop common beliefs about the possibilities for their business, their markets, their employees and themselves. Beliefs are powerful – some people will die rather than change them. When leadership harnesses common beliefs in an organization, their organizations are no longer playing roulette with their future, they are playing chess.*

One of the most vital aspects of your role as leader of the board is to ensure that this process is carried out well and at an appropriate frequency. There needs to be an ongoing consideration of trends and changes that are happening in the external environment, and indeed, in the company itself, but it is unlikely that any company would want to envision a completely new purpose every few years. Nevertheless, unexpectedly rapid changes in the political, economic, social or technological areas, or in competitor activity, may warrant a rethink of the company's vision. As chairman of the board, you need to be sensitive to these issues and lead the board as to the timing of any rethink.

In its publication *Standards for the Board*, the Institute of Directors identifies this broad task as 'Establish vision, mission and values'. The publication breaks it down into four separate sub-tasks and lists a number of indicators of good practice for each of them. Many chairmen will find it useful to refer to these indicators as an aid to leading the board into addressing this crucial task.

Experienced chairmen expressed the following views on some of the topics covered in this section

Sir Nigel Mobbs

The chairman's role in managing the board's agenda is vital to seeing that the main focus is strategic – looking ahead. There will, of course, be some monitoring but the emphasis here can be to see that the company has the management to make it happen and the financial muscle needed, as well as other matters such as seeking the right alliances and acquisitions. It is important to ensure that the company keeps its competitive edge and a focus on achieving the strategic objectives. When setting strategy, the chairman must be sensitive to bringing out the contributions of all the directors, where the views of the executive directors on the practicality of some of the ideas are important.

Linda Smith

The role that I think the board has is really to be setting strategic direction. It is very important for us in the health service because there are many things that can blow us off course. For instance, so many initiatives from government, so many budgetary difficulties, so many rises and falls in demand and supply, that it is very easy to get caught up in that sort of business. It is therefore very important that the board sees its role as to set a direction – not a slavish strategic plan, but a general direction around the questions, 'What are we trying to achieve?' and 'What sort of a health service do we want to promote and foster, encourage and help to develop locally?' And then we need to measure the ups and downs along the way in relation to that strategic direction. So that's a very important role of the board. Why I say that everyone contributes to it is because, if you are going in at the right level, if you are there at the beginning of that direction and you are taking your responsibility seriously there, then non-executive directors can have as much say as executive directors on that because you are starting with that initial decision.

This was a major refocusing strategically and we are doing this all the time; as things develop around us we are examining our role and changing, changing. We are at the hub of a whole system of local health delivery and we see our role now moving away from commissioning. Our role now is to make sure that there are connections within the system, so that individual patients can see a seamless service that works in an integrated way to meet their needs without duplication. Also, to work with local authorities to make sure that their responsibilities and ours are integrated well. We are at the heart of local healthcare and still struggling a little with our changing role, where we are having to let go of many responsibilities, while keeping accountability. And the more we can understand the difference and grapple with it, the more successful we will be. There is recognition that we can and should devolve and delegate responsibility but be very clear what we are accountable for and to whom, and to make sure that we find ways of keeping that accountability.

CORPORATE CULTURE AND VALUES

Every organization has a corporate culture – a set of values and a way of doing things that is implicitly understood and, hopefully, followed by those working in it. They might include such values as *probity, fairness, honesty, teamwork, quality, customer concern, fast response, professionalism, cost-consciousness, creativity, risk taking, competitiveness,* etc. This culture also circumscribes the way in which the company relates to other parties, or its stakeholders. As far as the employees are concerned, this culture will also influence the way they are encouraged, rewarded, criticized and promoted. It is underpinned by the ethical stance that the company adopts, or aspires to, which is dealt with in Chapter 4.

Corporate values will have a major influence on organizational behaviour. For everyone to believe in them they must be reflected in the way the leaders behave and act. If the board members are not seen to believe in these values in everything they do and say, their currency will be undermined. As chairman, you should insist that all your board colleagues honour this commitment at all times in word and deed.

It is clear that these fundamental value systems and standards must be sanctioned by the board of directors, which must also be satisfied that they are being upheld. But how does your board know that what people in the organization actually do reflects these values? Are you satisfied in relying solely on the chief executive and other executive directors to see to it that all is well in this area? If so, are audits carried out from time to time, some by independent organizations, and does the board see the report summaries and recommendations? Is the style of your board such that its members are encouraged to make random checks themselves? I have encountered directors who telephone the company as if they were a potential customer or one with a complaint to see how the matter is handled. Others call in unannounced at company facilities to get a spot check picture of attitudes and behaviours. If not handled with care, such random interventions can be counterproductive and in any case can never replace a more thorough, professional approach. You and your board should address these questions and decide what approach is best for your organization at a particular time.

Where values need to be changed over time, to embrace a changed future vision of the company, the broad issues should be discussed and agreed by the board and then translated into policy statements for the company and its employees to observe. However, it is usually wise for a process of consultation and involvement with employees to take place as a part of such changes. To ensure that these changes are addressed in a timely and proper way, the chairman and the chief executive/MD need to be sensitive to such issues. They should also have their fingers on the pulse of likely changes in stakeholder perceptions and expectations, as well as benchmarks of good practice in other organizations.

Although we may use the term 'corporate culture' to imply a single, all-embracing set of standards, values and attitudes, in practice there will be many sub-cultures existing together in the organization. Underpinning them all will be some fundamental values, to which all must subscribe. There should be a dynamic balance between the need for achieving a common purpose and the diverse behaviours and motivations of different groups within the company.

To illustrate four dimensions that a corporate culture might take, Bob Garratt (1996) adapts an analysis by Roger Harrison and Charles Handy (*The Gods of Management*) in his excellent book *The Fish Rots from the Head* in the following way:

1. ***Power culture.*** *The relationship between an all-powerful central figure, or small group, and the people in the divisions, business units, or work groups. The relationship is usually highly personalized and binary. You are either doing well or you are out. The power is bestowed in showers of*

gold or thunderbolts which vaporize the transgressor. The biggest 'sin' here is for individuals or groups on the periphery to gang up against the centre. Terrible retribution from the centre follows inevitably.

2. **Role culture.** *Symbolized as the front of a Grecian temple with order, calm, rationality and systems allowing everyone to know their place, what they can do and what they cannot do. It is about procedure and precision. Since I spend a lot of my time on 14-hour non-stop flights with Cathay Pacific Airways I am reassured that their engineering division is a Role culture and not a Power one. I like to think that the bolts are done up to the correct torque.*

3. **Task culture.** *This is the craftsmanship, technical excellence, and project-based culture. It demands delivery to quality, time and budget. There is a deliberate tension built into it – between getting the job done well, and developing the people who do the job so that they can learn to increase their effectiveness and efficiency. At present it is fashionable to strive for a Task culture whether you need one or not. It is not easy to install, and if the board's words and actions are out of synch over their desire for a more Task-based culture, then it is almost impossible to create.*

4. **People culture.** *This has lots of powerful individuals doing their work professionally without a lot of external management. It is found, for example, with barristers, TV directors and producers, hospital consultants, boards of directors, architects and software designers. It looks great from the outside, but just try and join it. Induction and inclusion are tough to the point of outright exclusion. These folk usually live in a carefully protected sealed bubble at the top, or centre, of the organization and protect their rights fiercely.*

For a board the question is which corporate culture, or range of cultures, is appropriate for their needs. A single, dominant culture need not be imposed on all parts of the enterprise – provided that the purpose, vision and values are clear to all and committed to. Different parts can adopt different cultures to reach the common end. It is a case of horses for courses.

Continuing with the airline example, it would be reasonable that engineering is essentially a Role culture, and so should administration, accounting and the administrative parts of personnel be. The customer-facing divisions should be essentially Task cultures, getting passengers and planes to their destinations on time, to quality and budget. The board, marketing, people development and finance functions should be People cultures. When crises hit there is likely to be an ultimate Power culture based on the dominant personality, or personalities, who will take the toughest decisions. This should be the board.

An experienced chairman expressed the following views on some of the topics covered in this section

Sir Nigel Mobbs

The questions of corporate culture and values are often essentially good housekeeping disciplines. The chairman's focus here is to ensure that the disciplines of the board are of the highest order and to see that there is a culture of honesty, transparency and integrity. It must start with the board subscribing to these values and ensuring that policies are in place that make them clear.

THINKING AND ACTING STRATEGICALLY

Strategic thinking

Directing an organization is essentially about doing just that – providing it with a sense of direction or purpose and ensuring its achievement. Having agreed a purpose and the goals that relate to it, the board must be equipped to formulate strategies that will be the basis for achieving those goals. This formulation requires a process (thinking), leading to the content (strategic plans). The board's main input will be in the thinking process that should occur before any planning takes place. The executive team can then put the plans together, based around the board's consideration of the likely options that might be available to the company. The subsequent step of the board approving the plans then becomes fairly straightforward.

The thinking done by the board in any organization should be at the highest conceptual level. This process will consider many possibilities, rejecting most of them and so deciding what not to do as well as what positive paths to take. These choices will be influenced by the concerns of practicability suggested mainly by the executive directors. But it is important not to be over-influenced by such issues, which can often stifle full consideration of new ideas and concepts. Strategies created by combining concepts with the practical will be far stronger and more likely to be achieved than those dominated by either constituent. The process requires the ability to take a 'helicopter' view, looking in all directions, but also to come down to earth to consider matters at close hand. Indeed, strategists should master the ability to alter the level of their thought and vision so as to focus in depth whenever the broader view suggests the wisdom of doing so.

The board must look outside the organization at the same time as it considers the internal constituents. Many companies fail to produce the strategies they need to succeed because they place too much emphasis on one of these dimensions and all but ignore the other. It is all too easy for some to be captivated by the possibilities out there in the big wide world, playing down the dangers and difficulties. On the other hand, many boards are mesmerized by the present strengths of the physical assets of the company or its dedicated and talented people, and limit their strategic thinking by that constraint.

It is essential to scan the external environment for opportunities, threats, trends and changes, but it is not enough just to do so. It is equally important to fully analyse the organization's capabilities and assets so that its strengths can be fully exploited and its weaknesses understood. Where weaknesses can be reduced or overcome, further opportunities can be considered that may have been discarded before. The board must keep both an outward and an inward perspective at the same time, contrasting one with the other and endeavouring to achieve a strategy that has them in balance by seeing each through an understanding of the other.

The quality of this strategic thinking process and the ability for it to take place depend on a number of factors. Perhaps the most important factor is the calibre and competence of the board members to carry it out effectively. Important considerations when selecting executive directors should be their ability to find out what needs to be known and to make judgements. These qualities are usually compromised or non-existent where their strengths are seen mainly in terms of what they know. At least some of the non-executive directors on a board should be chosen because, among other qualities and strengths, they have some imagination and creative flair. Too often one encounters boards where all the non-executive directors are seen as being there principally to play the role of overseeing management. This means that while they may be excellent at asking awkward questions about what has or has not happened and making judgements that are data-dependent, they are the last people to suggest anything new or make imaginative connections. If the executive directors also lack creativity and are rather hidebound, you will have little chance of developing winning strategies. This emphasizes once again the importance of the chairman's task of achieving a well-composed board.

I cannot over-stress how important it is for you to get a team around your board table that is able to conceive and agree strategies that will give your company a chance of prospering in the uncertain world of tomorrow. This requires a well-informed, experienced, outward-looking board that is realistic about resources, timescales and capabilities and which knows how obstacles might be overcome. At the same time it should encourage everyone in the organization to come forward with ideas that could lead to business development and diversification and make sure that they are properly considered. Without such a board, all your other endeavours will be compromised. We will return to the topic of board composition in a later chapter.

Strategy today

The business climate today is characterized by economic and corporate turbulence. Lead times and product life-cycles have been shortened dramatically. Capital now flows internationally, technology has changed the ways in which industries compete and new competitors keep emerging all the time.

Strategies now have to be flexible, adaptive and forever changing, although some consistency of intent is important. Companies have to learn to forget and ditch old habits. Many industry boundaries have to be redrawn and firms may have to compete differently to survive. The delineation of many markets needs to be redefined and new ways of accessing them explored. Strategic stretch replaces strategic fit, so that strategic architecture is more important than having a rigid, albeit solid, foundation. The situation is becoming more confused, iterative and even chaotic as all competitors face uncertainty ahead.

Thinkers such as Mintzberg, Peters, Hamel and Prahalad have argued that, given this turbulence, a traditional approach cannot possibly accommodate a statement of strategy relevant to current times.

Furthermore, it is argued that strategy formulation is no longer the preserve of the board and executive management. Instead, people in the entire company should share this responsibility.

Here are some thoughts on the subject of strategy by some business thinkers and practitioners:

It is not enough to work harder. Harder just doesn't cut it in a world of discontinuous innovation. It's not enough to get better. Companies are going to learn to get different – profoundly different.

In industry after industry I am seeing yesterday's business models being supplanted by radically new ways of doing business. This isn't process re-engineering, it's fundamental strategy innovation. 'Industry revolutionaries' are up-ending conventions and aggressive newcomers are challenging the orthodoxies of incumbents. In this topsy-turvy environment, irrelevancy may be a bigger risk than inefficiency.

It's a fact – over the past decade, newcomers have created the lion's share of new wealth in many industries. They've succeeded not by 'executing better', but by changing the rules of the game. In an increasingly non-linear world, only non-linear strategies will create new wealth. But in my work to date, there are few companies who I consider able to spawn imaginative, wealth-creating strategies. Strategy innovation can't be the once-a-decade product of a lone visionary, just as quality can't be the product of a lone artisan.

Any company that wants to survive in the turbulent new economy will have to learn how to harness the passion and imagination of every employee, in the quest for strategy innovation. It will have to learn how to smoothly manage the transition from old strategies to new strategies. It will have to learn to reinvent itself not once a decade, in the midst of a crisis, but year by year while still at the peak of performance. (Hamel, 1999)

If you see a bandwagon – it's too late! (Sir James Goldsmith)

Success is like winning a pinball game. You only win the chance to play another game. (Bill Gates)

Experience is great as long as the future resembles the past. If not experience can become downright dangerous. (Hamel, adapted)

Strategy entails making choices. Organizations cannot, any more, be all things to all people. Choices must be made. Likewise me-too strategies in today's hostile environment get punished. (Porter, 1985, adapted)

Any company that succeeds at restructuring and re-engineering, but fails to create the markets of the future, will find itself on a treadmill, trying to keep one step ahead of the steadily declining margins and profits of yesterday's businesses. (Hamel and Prahalad, 1994)

Indeed so overwhelmed are most chief executives by the heat and noise of the battle for survival and success that there is little opportunity for reflection on the wider issues involved. (Sir John Harvey-Jones)

The best strategy is one that can actually be carried out. (Sir John Harvey-Jones)

No company ever stops changing... each new generation must meet changes... the work of creating goes on. (Alfred P Sloan, 1986)

AGREEING OBJECTIVES, STRATEGIES AND PLANS

Goals and missions

Having created a vision of what the company will be like in the future, many companies make a written statement of what needs to be done to achieve the envisioned state. This statement of the company's 'mission', 'objectives' or 'goals' should be clear and easily understood by everyone in the organization – if employees don't think that it is credible or relevant to them it is unlikely to be achieved. The fashion for mission statements was led by many American companies and reached a degree of popularity some years ago. Scepticism for the idea arose in some circles because many mission statements appeared anodyne, unconvincing or trite. Perhaps because of this, many companies today avoid using the word 'mission' and merely state what the company's objective or goal is and then spell out what needs to be done, with some measurable targets relating to it. Such a goal is only tenable when it is underpinned by realistic strategies for its achievement.

Determining strategies

There are many different ways in which a board of directors can become involved in the process of determining the strategies for the organization. One way is to delegate the matter to the chief executive and his or her team and ask them to come forward with some strategic plans for the board to approve. This approach takes the view that since the executive directors know the business best, they are best qualified to come up with the best strategies. The board's role would therefore be confined to asking some questions about the assumptions behind the plans and then either approving them or asking for them to be re-examined or modified before finally approving them.

One danger of relying on the executive team to provide the strategies for the company is that they may be dominated by the chief executive/MD and his or her thinking, such that the full range of possible options is not considered thoroughly. Additionally, the executive team's thinking may be restricted and conditioned by the present day situation and past trends, and their assumptions may not be challenged properly. If this approach is adopted, the valuable insights, views and opinions of the non-executive directors, with their external perspective and breadth of experience, is lost at the essential conceptual stage. In any case, once the executives have put forward a plan, it is difficult for them to accept a radical rethink and to become properly engaged in the process themselves.

While it is true that drawing up strategic plans – indeed any plans – is a proper task for management, it is equally true that the board is the right body to think through the issues surrounding strategic options that might be available to the company, on which such plans are based. As a general principle, it is best to think things through first, then plan, then act and finally review the results of the actions. In this process, the board should delegate the planning and action, but be very much involved in the thinking and review processes. Clearly, the quality of the thinking that precedes the rest of the process is an essential key to the overall success. Thinking through the matters of where the company should go and how it should get there are the board's most important tasks. This affords the best opportunity for the directors to bring their experience, wisdom and diverse viewpoints to bear on the issues involved, so as to inform any related plans that management subsequently draws up.

It is better, therefore, if the whole board thinks through all the options and possibilities in an open way before any real planning is even considered. Ideas and views from any relevant people in the organization should ideally inform these options. This is therefore the recommended best practice. Where the board is all-executive, the chairman's role will essentially be to have the board stand back from the current situation and be stimulated to think strategically, often with the involvement of an external facilitator.

Where the board includes a number of non-executive directors, perhaps with disparate backgrounds and substantially different experience profiles, their combination of business acumen, philosophical perspectives, special knowledge and practical experience can add a degree of richness to the board's discussions on strategic matters which would be denied an all-executive board. To gain this benefit, it is important to have appointed non-executive directors of an appropriate calibre and for the chairman to lead the board in a way that draws on the potential of their experience and viewpoints, while interacting with the views and business experience of the executive directors.

Most boards today take time out to meet in a fairly informal way to think through the strategic options that the company might take and to agree the broad strategy to be adopted. This is often done away from the business premises over one or two days. Some boards invite senior people from the organization and others to join them for at least some of the proceedings, to provide an extra richness of ideas and expertise to draw upon. Many involve a consultant specializing in strategy work to throw down some challenges, question assumptions and provide rigour and thoroughness to the process. Although an annual session like this is quite common, an increasing number of boards are finding that a more frequent reassessment of strategy is necessary in the fast-moving, unpredictable environment that their business operates in now.

Another approach being adopted by boards to help keep a sharp strategic focus in a fast-changing world is to have a meeting once each quarter dedicated solely to strategic matters. At these meetings, all the assumptions on which the strategy was previously based are reconsidered. Their validity and continuing relevance are rigorously questioned and ongoing likely trends reassessed. Particular attention is paid to matters relating to the external environment that could affect the business, including competitor factors. However, internal issues are also reviewed, particularly those involving adapting to the consequences of change. This practice recognizes and accommodates the need to have a flexible strategic approach in many business areas today. It does not mean taking a fundamental change of direction every few months, but facilitates sensible changes of pace and fine-tuning. It also provides a regular procedure for the board to watch and consider new opportunities and threats, and recognize when a major reassessment of broad strategy may be needed, based on what is happening externally rather than by the calendar.

Every director should be alert to new developments and trends that might affect the company or provide opportunities for its advancement. However, the relevance and potential to the business of these developments and trends can easily remain unrecognized until they are obvious – and too late.

Ideally, the board needs to have a very sharp awareness of what is happening in each of the external domains – political, physical, economic, social, technological, geographical, market, competitor, supplier, shareholder, stakeholder. The 'multiview' approach provides that sharpness by making it the special responsibility of each director to be acutely aware of one or two of these domains specifically, and to keep the board informed of any changes or trends from them that might be significant. It is rather like each director watching out in a specific direction using radar and a telescope, rather than everyone trying to look in all directions at once with bare eyes. Taking on this responsibility on behalf of the board creates an obligation on each director not to let down the team, which can be very powerful. You may find that adopting this 'multiview' approach will help your board to ensure that it remains more acutely aware of what is happening externally to the company on a broad scale.

Plans and targets

Any strategies that the board agrees will result in a many-faceted plan covering a range of factors. Assumptions will be made about such matters as the markets, competitors, the economic and political environment, finance, the people in the organization, availability of the necessary physical assets and the soundness of the expected competitive advantage. Across the timescale of the plan there should be targets relating to these assumptions that are agreed by the board, by which achievement of the strategy can be judged and monitored.

Deciding what these targets should be and how and at what frequency their achievement should be monitored is clearly very important. The board needs early warning if achievement of the plan is likely to be jeopardized, due either to internal factors or changes in the assumptions that were made about the external environment, the market, competitors, etc. Yet many boards pay scant attention to deciding these targets, often relying on the planning process itself, essentially carried out by the management, to produce them. Good board chairmanship should ensure that there is ample time allocated for the whole board to discuss these matters thoroughly and comprehensively. The kind of questions to be addressed at such a session are:

- What factors that are external to the company should be monitored?
- What internal factors should be monitored?
- How should the monitoring be carried out and by whom?
- At what frequency should each factor be monitored?
- What degree of variance from the plan assumptions would warrant reporting to the board?
- What forms should the reports take and who should make them?

Some of the factors to be monitored by the board will be based on numerical data, but many will be expressed in the form of trends and of 'softer' variables such as competitor and marketing activity or the degree of employees' enthusiasm to changing work practices. If these matters are thought through with care at the outset, unpleasant surprises can be avoided and everyone in the organization can be aware of what is important to the plan's achievement. The board only really needs to know if something important is likely to go wrong that may then require some new decisions to be made about the strategic direction of the company.

An experienced chairman expressed the following views on some of the topics covered in this section

Linda Smith

I would agree that focusing on strategic issues is our role, but how do we do this? It's obvious that if we are having open board meetings and we are performance managing and we are looking at accountability, and we have standard items on the agenda, then we can't always focus properly on the bigger strategic issues anticipating the future and really think them through. So we do that on board away-days that give us a chance, several times a year, to think around, 'Where is this heading?' We would have one of these sessions to consider any major new government initiatives or changes. For instance, what is the role of the Health Authority and how will it change now that we have Primary Care Groups and a move towards Primary Care Trusts? We considered these matters over several away-days and as a result have since restructured completely the Health Authority, including replacing two directors.

We do have very specific goals and strategies and plans, but some of it is quite 'big picture' and some of it is constantly developing and changing. Where I think we are not so good and need to pay more attention is in anticipating what might be coming at us and making sure that we are constantly adjusting and scanning. This requires that we are constantly looking outside, looking at government policies, looking at the wider picture, looking at social trends and political mood, and anticipating the likely effect on our organization. That is the backdrop of what we do and therefore we need to be quite good at scanning and understanding that and sharing some of that, as a board. Knowing what these timescales are that you should be considering and working to is also very important. Within that, one of the issues that is quite important is that, as things change, it is vital that we ask the questions, 'Does the organization have the capability and what are you doing, executive directors, to develop the capability we will need?'

Our reorganization of the Health Authority started off with the board considering the role of the Health Authority in the future, where it was going and what the implications of that were. One consideration was what sort of organization structure might be required, with the board guiding the chief executive to look beyond structure to the issues of the skills and competencies that would be needed, the sort of values that the organization should have and how to develop these. Because the executive directors were very much implicated in any changes, it was perhaps rather tricky for the non-executive directors to take the leading role there, whereas in other matters it is usually a more shared role. That was quite an important juncture for us. I suppose that's the classic board role really. It's to see the changes, to say that things have to change, to put the criteria in place, to pay attention to the things it was felt needed to be acted upon and then empowering the organization and letting them get on with it. Then to possibly ask the questions, 'Have you gone far enough? How is this now shaping up? How are you developing the organizational capability to meet the future? Is it being done?'

CHAPTER CHECKLIST

Here are some questions you might ask yourself in connection with the matters covered in this chapter before you plan any consequent action:

- Does your board take time out periodically to envision what the organization should be like in the future?
- ... and what values and corporate culture might be appropriate?
- Do all your directors behave and act in a way that upholds and reflects the company's understood values?
- ... and does the board satisfy itself that everyone in the organization is upholding those values?
- Are you sensitive to likely changes in stakeholder perceptions and expectations, as well as good practice standards?
- ... and does your board agree changes that should be made consequently?
- ... and are policy statements produced or changed to reflect these new values and standards?
- Does your board's strategic thinking balance both the outward and inward perspectives?
- ... and the conceptual with the practical?
- Is a statement of the organization's goals or objectives produced in written form for all to see?

- Does your board think through strategic options in an open way before any strategic plans are drawn up?
- Does your board reassess the company's strategy regularly in the light of current trends?
- … and is the frequency of doing so determined by external events and trends rather than the calendar?
- Have each of your directors taken on the responsibility of keeping the board informed of changes and trends happening in specific external domains?
- Does your board decide what targets should be used to monitor achievement of strategic plans?
- … and do they include expressions of 'soft' variables and trends as well as data-based factors?
- Is your board really up to the job of ensuring the company's future prosperity?

3

Monitoring the enterprise

DELEGATING PROPER AUTHORITY

One of the key tasks of a board is to delegate to the managers of the company the authority they need. The scope of this authority will vary from one organization to another, but it is essential that the board itself does not get bogged down in operational matters and post-mortems on day-to-day issues. All too frequently one sees boards that spend much of their time at board meetings discussing and dissecting matters that have little or no bearing on the destiny of the organization, its reputation or the safeguarding of its interests. Yet this is where the board's focus should be.

Where should the line be drawn?

Perhaps the single most important decision that you can get your board to make is to determine those matters that it should and should not decide upon. Once this fundamental decision has been made, you may be pleasantly surprised how relatively easy it is for you to have the directors concentrate on their essential role, while clearly leaving to the management those matters that more properly fall into their domain. This resolution will also help executive directors to separate clearly their roles as directors and managers.

What are the matters that should be the preserve of the board alone and which should be delegated to management? Although there are no universal, definitive answers to these questions, I can suggest some general rules and lines of guidance that will allow your board to determine what might be appropriate in your case.

As a broad rule, the board should reserve to itself decisions that will determine:

- the long-term prosperity, viability, security and reputation of the organization;
- policies governing the way the organization is perceived and treats others:
- relations with shareholders (or other higher bodies in cases where there are no shareholders);
- policies covering material financial matters and commitments, statutory obligations, compliance, relations with relevant stakeholders, probity and ethical matters;
- matters concerning the board and senior management;
- authority levels.

Set out below is an example of a statement of a board's reserved powers. It is not a universally comprehensive list and some of the matters included may not apply to your board or organization. Nevertheless, it does indicate the sorts of topics that many boards would include and could be a useful starting point when you get your board to agree its own reserved powers list. The board might find it helpful to consider any relevant matters in the Memorandum and Articles of Association and any other prescriptive documents when drawing up such a list.

Example of a board's reserved powers list

Strategic and financial matters

Considering and agreeing:

- the company's purpose, vision, mission, goals and objectives;
- strategies and strategic plans;
- annual budgets;
- regular reviews of performance against budgets and plans;
- any matter that would have a material effect on the company's financial position, liabilities, future strategy or reputation;
- major capital projects in excess of (x value);
- capital expenditure in excess of budgets;
- changes to the company's capital structure;
- significant changes in accounting, risk management, capital and treasury policies and practices, including foreign exchange exposures;
- significant changes to the company's financial and management control systems;
- capital expenditure, disposals, acquisitions and joint ventures above the authority levels delegated to the chief executive/MD;
- the establishment and annual review of such delegated authority levels;
- contracts not in the ordinary course of business and material contracts in the ordinary course of business;
- net borrowings in excess of peak budgeted or forecasted levels.

Shareholder matters

Considering and agreeing:

- dividends to shareholders;

- financial statements, including interim and Annual Reports and Accounts;
- circulars and prospectuses to shareholders, including listing arrangements and those convening general meetings, except circulars of a routine nature;
- review of auditor's letter of recommendations.

Recommending to shareholders:

- changes to the Memorandum and Articles of Association;
- reappointment or change of auditors;
- approval of audit fee;
- approval of auditor's engagement letter and scope of audit;
- the issue of ordinary and preference shares;
- share option schemes.

Board and senior executive matters

Considering and agreeing:

- appointment and removal of directors and company secretary, including those of subsidiaries;
- powers, roles and duties delegated to individual directors, including the chairman, chief executive/MD and finance director;
- remuneration and terms of appointment of directors and senior executives, including bonus arrangements, share options, pensions and contracts of employment;
- terms of reference and membership of board committees;
- material changes in pension scheme rules;
- liability insurance arrangements for directors and officers of the company.

Principles

Considering, agreeing and reviewing compliance with:

- contracts, laws, statutory obligations and regulations;
- company policies on probity, and ethics;

- the company Code of Conduct;
- company policies on employment matters;
- company policies on matters concerning the physical environment;
- company policies on communications and reputation management;
- company policies on risk management and internal control.

It is good practice to draw up a complementary list to the board's reserved powers, specifying unambiguously what powers and levels of authority have been delegated to the chief executive/MD. The board should pass a formal resolution confirming the delegation of these powers so that the executive concerned has a clear mandate and authority. This approach also helps to avoid problems due to omission or misunderstanding and helps executive directors more clearly differentiate their board and management roles.

An experienced chairman expressed the following views on some of the topics covered in this section

Sir Nigel Mobbs

Within the board there need to be clear areas of delegation and discretion to avoid overlaps and ambivalence in who is responsible for what. This comes down to delegating proper authority, essentially. Our board has a detailed schedule setting out the procedures for carrying out certain tasks and areas and limits of authority delegated by the board, so that everyone knows where they stand. The schedule lists out where the limitations are and avoids confusion. All directors have a copy and one is available at board meetings too, for reference when necessary.

SEEING THE WOOD THROUGH THE TREES

Since the board has ultimate responsibility for the viability and performance of the organization, how can it be certain that it knows what is happening? The answer is, of course, that it cannot possibly know everything that is going on all the time and should not try to. On the other hand, there must be a high degree of confidence that the organization's policies are being followed, targets and budgets are being met and that the company's reputation and assets are in good order. Just as important is the confidence that the strategic evolution of the company is taking place as agreed and that the assumptions that the plans were based upon are still likely to be valid.

In reviewing the performance of the company, some boards of directors all too easily slip into management mode and discuss in detail what has happened, what may happen and how to make changes as a consequence. While it is right and proper for the executive directors to do this in their roles as managers, that is for another time and place, with the chief executive / MD orchestrating the discussion. The board's main concerns here are that the company's affairs are being conducted as they should be and that results are much as expected – and if they are not, what steps are being taken to put matters right and what might be the consequences. Only where the likely consequences might compromise the company's reputation or security, or require a re-evaluation of strategic decisions previously taken, might the chairman judge that further consideration by the board is appropriate.

Those chairmen who are also the chief executive / MD of the company (including many who call themselves 'executive chairman') often have particular difficulties during board meetings in keeping the board focused on directing the organization. Especially, this can be the case when all the directors are executives. Since the executive directors spend most of their time with the chairman and chief executive / MD in their executive roles, it is all too easy for him or her to 'switch hats' without realizing it. The executive directors will then come to regard this everyday practice of mixing board and management matters as normal.

If you are responsible for fulfilling both these roles, be particularly careful to separate them and to make it clear which role you are playing, particularly during board meetings. When dealing with the monitoring of management items on the agenda, make sure that any consequential action is addressed away from the board meeting, where you will be clearly acting in your executive role.

Effective monitoring of the company by the board is a quite complex matter, covering a number of areas and potentially a large number of topics. Yet it is important that the board does not get involved in too much detail, particularly of an historical nature, while having confidence that the company is on track and under prudent control. It must keep its focus on the big picture, despite having a spectrum of more detailed matters potentially available to consider. I have likened this to 'seeing the wood through the trees' How can you help your board to obtain this balance? One key issue is to ensure that the monitoring process is effective, without drawing the board into spending time on excessive detail. To get this right it is important that the board addresses the appropriate performance criteria and is happy with the quality of the management controls that underpin the information being monitored.

An experienced chairman expressed the following views on some of the topics covered in this section

Dennis Woods

A key to the effective monitoring of what is going on is to have executive directors who are not up to their eyeballs in day-to-day matters and problems. They must have good people they can rely on and delegate things to others. They must also build teams, have good succession planning and cross-training between departments. The chief executive/MD must see that there is strength being built into the organization all the way through – making sure that there are no weaknesses in the foundations or bricks out of place. In the end, the success of the board's decisions often depends on the effectiveness of how people in the organization are managed and what they see as their priorities. Our biggest danger is complacency – taking our eye off the ball, taking the business for granted. I've learnt this the hard way and I don't mind telling the staff about the mistakes they and I have made – we must all learn from mistakes.

AGREEING PERFORMANCE INDICATORS AND CONTROLS

The criteria used for monitoring achievement

The benefits of taking a disciplined, top-down, periodic view of those factors that are vital to the future and ongoing prosperity as well as reputation of the enterprise cannot be overstated, even with an all-executive board. This prevents the confusion that occurs when these factors are mixed in with the myriad of other performance factors that managers are confronted with from day to day. It is therefore important to ensure that the criteria used are appropriate for the task.

Many boards tend to look at too many measures – usually figures giving accounting information, each requiring some evaluation or judgement as to its relevance. Such an approach can be unnecessarily time-consuming and often misses a review of important issues that are not of a strictly financial nature. Instead, I would recommend the assumption of a more disciplined approach which, once adopted, will make it easier for you to keep the discussion focused on the issues that are of proper concern to your board.

To do this, the board must discuss and decide a) what specific items it would be appropriate to monitor, b) in which form, and c) how frequently. At the same time it can be agreed who will be responsible for presenting the relevant information and reporting on it if required. This list of items should be reviewed for continuing relevance annually or whenever a significant change of strategy is adopted, and modified if appropriate. In the meantime, since every board member has been party to agreeing this list, you can and should insist that the board strictly addresses these monitoring criteria. Only very special, exceptional reasons should be allowed for deviating from them occasionally.

In drawing up the list of criteria to be used, be sure to include 'soft' issues, where periodic internal or independent audits can be called for, such as:

- customer satisfaction;
- employee morale and motivation;
- legal and regulatory compliance;

- protection of key assets;
- compliance with company policies;
- innovation; etc.

After all, the board should primarily focus on monitoring the underlying health of the company, rather than the financial results for last month, meaningful though they undoubtedly are. The executive directors and other members of the management team should address these more day-to-day issues at their separate review meetings. It is also important for the board to monitor achievement against many of the milestones in the strategic evolution of the company.

Keep the number of financially based measures the board considers to a minimum, by identifying those relatively few primary ones that indicate what is happening or likely to occur. This will enable the secondary issues, which are really consequential to the others, to be ignored with confidence. Wherever possible, look at variances from what was expected to happen (eg, budget or forecast) rather than the quantum itself. The underlying question is, 'Are we on track?', which is easily answered if the allowable variances have already been established. Also, it is often useful to consider trends that may indicate underlying potential changes, which may need to be addressed. These trend characteristics are usually best presented in graphical form.

The validity and reliability of information presented

If the board is to have confidence in the monitoring process, there must be credence that the information it sees is valid and timely. The integrity and relevance of this information in turn rely on the soundness of the internal controls and their supporting systems. It follows therefore that the board must be satisfied that they are sound.

Some organizations test their internal control procedures by having them audited by either internal or external teams. Besides being good practice, such an audit can provide the directors with independent reports on the integrity and scope of the procedures, systems and outputs. It also affords the board an opportunity to be satisfied that the procedures are adequately resourced. Even without an in-depth audit, a thorough review should be regularly undertaken.

Overall, you should assume the responsibility for ensuring that the monitoring information given to your board is always up to date and always presented in sufficient time to allow directors to adequately prepare themselves for board meetings. The quality of the board's decisions will be the better for it.

Monitoring the company's achievements against expectations is all very well, but there can be a danger of becoming complacent, particularly when results appear to be unfolding as expected. After all, the expectations were agreed on the basis of a number of assumptions that were considered likely to occur. A question that should be asked periodically is, 'Are those assumptions still valid and likely to remain so?' Some of those assumptions will concern the many dimensions of the environment in which the company operates. Others will pertain to resources. The factors to be considered might include:

- trends in the marketplace;
- competitor activity;
- the regulatory regime;
- economic factors;
- the availability of technology;
- employee matters;
- the availability of physical resources;
- the availability of financial resources, etc.

It therefore makes sense for the board to re-examine the validity and continuing relevance of the factors it considers pertinent to review in this context. The frequency of such reviews will depend on the circumstances of the company and the business activities that it is engaged in.

One way to help ensure that these reviews are effective is for you to ask each director (sometimes just the executive directors) to take special responsibility for keeping the board informed about significant real or likely future changes in one or more of these factors. This can take the form of either a formal written report or a verbal presentation, which should include comments on how they think the changes might affect the expected outcomes. You can then encourage the whole board to debate the report, with the other directors asking questions and offering their own views on the subject.

Giving directors these special responsibilities, open to peer review, often ensures that the whole board is more thoroughly aware, on a broader front, than it would otherwise be. On the other hand, you must encourage all of the directors to be generalists, with interest and awareness across the whole spectrum of the company's affairs, and not blinkered specialists.

Experienced chairmen expressed the following views on some of the topics covered in this section

Sir Nigel Mobbs

I think one must have the usual system of budgets, forecasts and primary performance indicators, which are bound to be mostly financial, plus the reporting of key statistics and other indicators, such as risk, bad debts, etc. These will vary from company to company and must be decided by the board. New ones will be added from time to time, but these will usually be specific to the business. The board must be regularly briefed as to progress and performance against these indicators and discuss them by exception. The volume of data isn't important, it is whether you can see positive or adverse trends – don't let the board drown in data!

Linda Smith

The performance management role is not going to be easy – there's more to it than only performance managing the things that are easy to measure or where you can tick boxes. It's about really understanding how the system should be qualitatively improved and what would be the indicators that would tell you that. I am very much someone who is a facilitator of processes myself, so my role as chair I see very much as a process worker. So knowing what the processes should be, while all the time improving how you performance manage and how you get to manage the right things in the right way, understanding the whole issue of developing accountability and giving away responsibility – that is something you don't get to, you constantly have to work with it. And making sure that you are constantly working with it is I think what the board should be doing. And setting the tone for all that – what the board pays attention to is as significant in a way as whether it gets the answers right or not. If it pays attention to things it makes it clear what the important things are and enables other people to as well. It sets the context and the culture for making sure that people within the system, outside the organization, are able to play their roles and do the things they need to do.

HANDLING SUCCESSES AND FAILURES

The competence of management

Having competent people managing the organization is clearly a crucial factor in giving the board confidence that the company is likely to be on track and under control. After all, this is a prerequisite for delegating the necessary power and having the trust and understanding that are essential features of sound delegation. If delegation is to be effective, there must be competent people to delegate to who have the time and resources to carry out the tasks required. For this to be done successfully, everyone in the organization must be sure of what they must do and be well managed and led. These requisites apply in any management context and delegation by the board is no exception. That is the main reason why the board should be satisfied with the ability and competence of the management and the adequacy of the resources that will be at their disposal. The board should also be concerned that managers and others working in the organization are well motivated and developed and that there is proper acknowledgement of both good and bad performance.

The directors must have full confidence in the senior management, since good senior managers will usually ensure that they are supported by competent, well-motivated people at more junior levels. Many boards have a process to consider all senior management appointments, rather than leaving the matter solely to the chief executive/MD. This has the advantage of bringing the combined experience and judgement of all or a number of directors to bear on the choice of the key managers on whom the board must rely. It can also be a safeguard against favouritism, either real or imagined. In some companies there is a policy that all senior management appointments just below board level are endorsed by every director, in recognition of the need for this universal confidence.

The key question is whether the management will be up to the job of delivering the achievement of the future strategic performance that the board has agreed, in the timescale allowed. This requirement may be demanding in some quite different ways to the current and past situations, calling on different skills, knowledge and capabilities. The board should be both reflective and realistic in assessing these capabilities – a time to stand back and take a long, hard look at how the achievement of a new strategic plan will be managed and the necessary resources applied.

It is all too easy to just leave it all to the chief executive/MD, with only his or her reassurance, as some boards do. But the process of all the board members having an opportunity to explore what the chief executive/MD has in mind and satisfying themselves of its likely adequacy is a good discipline for all concerned. One of the outcomes of this procedure will be the highlighting of events on the critical path and potential weaknesses and when they are likely to occur or become critical. As chairman, you should note these and ensure that they are reported on specifically at appropriate times.

Another of the essential elements of effective delegation is trust. In the case of the board delegating some of its powers to the chief executive/MD, there must be a very high degree of confidence in the competence, ability and integrity of that person. This confidence must be maintained at all times for that essential trust to stay secure, and your close relationship with the chief executive/MD can help in keeping him or her sensitive to the vulnerable aspects of that confidence.

Although the board will entrust much to the chief executive/MD, it is at all times responsible for what happens within the company and cannot abdicate that responsibility. This fact is central to the requirement of the board to monitor the activities of the company and its performance. Clearly, an over-reliance on the word of the chief executive/MD, in terms of the ability of management, the application of resources and the activities and performance of the company, would be an abdication of the board's overall responsibility. It would also place too much power in the hands of one person. On the other hand, the chief executive/MD must be given a large measure of authority and the necessary scope and freedom of action to get the job done successfully, requiring as it does a high degree of trust on the part of the board.

Accommodating these two positions and getting the balance between them right is a task for all boards and a matter on which the chairman must focus. Much will depend on the personalities of those concerned and the style of the board itself. Changes of circumstance, such as the appointment of a new chief executive/MD or chairman, or a major change of the company's direction or constitution, can afford opportunities to consider whether a different balance might be appropriate, at least for a trial period.

A climate for achievement

Whatever methods of delegation are used, the most successful usually attempt to relate the perceived personal success of each individual in the organization to the overall achievement of company objectives. In this way, positive or negative feedback and the endorsement or disapproval of actions and behaviour are strongly contingent upon the degree of compliance with company policies, objectives and goals. Such a climate influences who is promoted and developed as well as levels of financial reward. It also affects the way people are treated by their peers and by their seniors in the organization. The creation and maintenance of a culture that promotes such a climate of achievement is often a key factor in effective delegation and the achievement of company performance.

Ideally, the management style should be open, with quick, honest and clear communication that engenders constructive feedback. Everyone in the organization should understand how they can carry out their work in a way that will help meet the aims and objectives of the company. That is not to say that all directors can or should be involved with all such matters on a continuous basis, even though executive directors would be so in their own management domains. But you can encourage the board to insist that a culture or climate exists within the organization that fosters such a paradigm and to be satisfied that it is so.

One way of achieving such a climate, which has been very effective for many companies, is to adopt a 'balanced scorecard' approach, originally suggested by Kaplan and Norton (1996) in the United States. A balanced scorecard measures what results must be achieved by those working in the company, in order to meet the stated objectives or mission that the board has agreed. It comprises a quantified set of performance measures, normally bespoke for the particular company, the achievement of which can be appraised objectively. These measures would go beyond financial performance requirements, and might typically cover such areas as:

- financial performance (sales, contribution, profit, ROCE, cash flow);
- business process performance (costs, productivity, quality, timeliness);
- market performance (market share, customer satisfaction, customer loyalty);
- employee performance (employee satisfaction, length of service, demonstrated best practices);
- innovation performance (added value improvement, sales from new products/services, rate of improvement index, employee suggestions).

Whether this approach or another that works already is adopted, your board needs to be satisfied that a climate for achieving the required performance exists throughout the company. If there are doubts, then perhaps you should persuade your chief executive/MD that the matter should be discussed at a board meeting in the near future.

An experienced chairman expressed the following views on some of the topics covered in this section

Sir Nigel Mobbs

On the whole, handling success isn't too difficult – most people probably don't think they are praised enough. I'm not a great believer in exceptionally praising people for doing what they are actually supposed to be doing. But then one must be careful at how one deals with failure. In some cases it may be due to a failure of the business environment, rather than of the way the business is managed – so benchmarking against other companies is relevant. Then, I think one should allow one error before being heavy-handed, unless the error is so patently stupid. If a myriad of errors starts to build up, one shouldn't be too patient. We do have a 'no surprises rule' at our board meetings and I have a short meeting with the executive directors beforehand that I find helpful.

CHAPTER CHECKLIST

Here are some questions you might ask yourself in connection with the matters covered in this chapter before you plan any consequent action:

- Do you ensure that your board does not get bogged down in operational matters and day-to-day issues?
- Will your board agree a list of powers it will reserve for itself?
- ... and a complementary list specifying the powers and levels of authority delegated to the chief executive/MD?
- If you are both chairman and chief executive/MD, do you ensure that any action that is a consequence of the board's monitoring process is dealt with outside the board meetings?
- Does your board periodically take a disciplined, top-down view of the performance factors that are crucial to the ongoing prosperity and reputation of the company?
- ... including milestones' marking its strategic evolution?

- ... and address only those when monitoring company performance at board meetings (with occasional exceptions)?
- ... and do they include criteria relating to 'soft' issues?
- ... that are periodically audited?
- Are financial performance measures kept to essentials and largely focused on variances – 'Are we on track'?
- ... and are trends considered too?
- Is a thorough review of the internal control procedures undertaken regularly, perhaps by an audit team?
- ... and are the consequent reports considered by the board and acted upon where necessary?
- Do you ensure that the monitoring information given to your board is sent out ahead of board meetings but is always up to date?
- Does your board periodically review the continuing validity of assumptions previously made concerning external and internal factors?
- ... and does each director have special responsibility for keeping the board informed about real and likely changes in these factors?
- Does your board influence the standards of competence required of those selected for senior management positions?
- ... and does it insist that a climate exists within the organization that encourages staff to work so that the company's aims and objectives are met?
- ... as well as their own?

4

Shareholders, stakeholders and other concerns

CONSIDERING RISK AND REPUTATION

What risks should you be taking?

Most strategically related decisions facing a board of directors will involve an element of risk for the company. Of all the decisions taken by the board, those of a strategic nature will usually contain the greatest element of judgement and guesswork – after all, nobody knows what the future may hold. The greater the complexity or degree of uncertainty contained in the judgements to be made, the greater the risk. The relative scale of the commitment to be made will also compound the scale of the consequences of the risk. And yet, obtaining future competitive advantage must inevitably involve a degree of uncertainty, and therefore risk.

Some companies fall by the wayside because their boards have not been prepared to take the degree of perceived risk that the situation facing them required – faint hearts seldom win competitions. On the other hand, many companies have failed because wrong decisions involving a high degree of uncertainty and risk were taken, requiring a commitment of resources on a large scale. Sometimes the high-risk decisions were the right ones, but there was a subsequent failure to carry them through effectively in the timescale required. The failure here would centre on judgements about the adequacy and timeliness of applying the resources that were needed. This often boils down to the company not having enough good people, well led and committed, with the time and resources available to produce the results required. In either case, the key failure lies in the board's inability to make the key judgements correctly, including those concerned with overseeing the successful implementation of change.

Even where commercial and market related risks are well judged, companies may incur severe problems or fail because other potential risks have not been adequately foreseen and controlled. Such risks can relate to areas such as financial, legal, compliance and probity matters and those that affect the reputation of the organization.

Being in business is about assuming risks, not avoiding them. On the other hand, risks to the business should be minimized wherever possible. Clearly, every board will have its own particular attitude towards risk taking – that disposition is part of its unique culture. As its chairman, you must have concern for the appropriateness of your board's disposition towards risk in present circumstances. One definition of risk is that it equates to 'what you stand to lose, minus what you can afford to lose', and this is likely to change with the times. When the competitive situation in the marketplace is changing or the company's financial position is markedly different compared with what it was, perhaps a different attitude towards commercial risk is justified. If so, it could be worthwhile having your board discuss the matter and agreeing that a change of approach is necessary. Such a consensus will equip you to guide future decision making appropriately, whenever entrenched perspectives are still being adopted. However, changing the board's composition, involving bringing new people onto the board with suitable personal outlooks, may be the only way to bring about genuine and effective change in the board's attitude toward risk.

The management and control of risk

In the complex business world of today, risk from covert activities such as fraud and overt eventualities such as poor judgement or ineffective controls are manifest. This complexity is compounded by the increasing legal and regulatory pressure to make directors personally accountable for the activities of the company's staff. How can your board be sure that such risks are quantified and understood, and is there proper and adequate control and management of risk?

This is a very complex and wide-reaching subject in itself, which is covered comprehensively and in a practical way by Robin Kendall (1998) in his book *Risk Management for Executives*. Although some of the topics are of particular application to companies in the financial services sector, most will apply universally. Kendall recommends the establishment of a special committee reporting to the board of directors, or in small companies the chairman or owner, to oversee risk management. This body must have both independence and authority, without diminishing the role of management. Kendall makes the point that risk in business can occur in many ways and identifies five broad areas of risk that should be addressed, under the following headings: market risk, credit risk, operational risk, legal risk and miscellaneous.

Whatever approach is adopted, the board and indeed management should not get so bogged down in detail that the bigger picture becomes blurred. Clearly, most effort and time should be spent on the control and management of those risks that are likely to have the greatest impact on the business. If the 80:20 rule applies to risk as it does in most other domains, then it is worth identifying the largest potential risks so that the management and control effort can be concentrated there. One of the most important functions of the directors in this area is in using their collective judgement to assess the degree and importance of each particular risk to identify where the most effort should be directed. The value of such an assessment process is best achieved by having an open discussion about each level and area of risk, including consideration of the aggregation of risks to the company as a whole.

When considering the internal control and management of risk applying to companies, perhaps the definitive reference on the subject is the *Guidance on Internal Control (The Turnbull Guidance)*, which was published in 2005 by the Financial Reporting Council and is required reading for all directors of listed companies. Directors of other organizations who want to take this important matter of risk management more seriously should also consider the recommendations. (See www.frc.org.uk/images/uploaded/documents.)

The narrative details the importance of internal control and risk management and of the maintenance and review of a sound system of internal control. It states that it is for the board to decide if it is appropriate to use board committees. The decision will depend on factors such as the size and composition of the board, the scale, diversity and complexity of the company's operations and the nature of the significant risks the company faces. An appendix lists some useful questions that the board may wish to discuss with management when assessing the effectiveness of the risk and control processes; these are reproduced below. The preamble points out that the questions are not intended to be exhaustive and will need to be tailored to the particular circumstances of the company concerned:

1. Risk assessment
   - Does the company have clear objectives and have they been communicated so as to provide effective direction to employees on risk assessment and control issues? For example, do objectives and related plans include measurable performance targets and indicators?
   - Are the significant internal and external operational, financial, compliance and other risks identified and assessed on an ongoing basis? These are likely to include the principal risks identified in the Operational and Financial Review. (Significant risks may, for example, include those related to market, credit, liquidity, technological, legal, health, safety and environmental, reputation, and business probity issues.)
   - Is there a clear understanding by management and others within the company of what risks are acceptable to the board?

2. Control environment and control activities
   - Does the board have clear strategies for dealing with the significant risks that have been identified? Is there a policy on how to manage these risks?
   - Do the company's culture, code of conduct, human resource policies and performance reward systems support the

business objectives and risk management and internal control system?

- Does senior management demonstrate, through its actions as well as its policies, the necessary commitment to competence, integrity and fostering a climate of trust within the company?
- Are authority, responsibility and accountability defined clearly such that decisions are made and actions taken by the appropriate people? Are the decisions and actions of different parts of the company appropriately coordinated?
- Does the company communicate to its employees what is expected of them and the scope of their freedom to act? This may apply to areas such as customer relations; service levels for both internal and outsourced activities; health, safety and environmental protection; security of tangible and intangible assets; business continuity issues; expenditure matters; accounting; financial and other reporting.
- Do people in the company (and in its providers of outsourced services) have the knowledge, skills and tools to support the achievement of the company's objectives and to manage effectively risks to their achievement?
- How are processes/controls adjusted to reflect new or changing risks, or operational deficiencies?

3. Information and communication
   - Do management and the board receive timely, relevant and reliable reports on progress against business objectives and the related risks that provide them with the information, from inside and outside the company, needed for decision making and management review purposes? This could include performance reports and indicators of change, together with qualitative information such as on customer satisfaction, employee attitudes, etc.
   - Are information needs and related information systems reassessed as objectives and related risks change or as reporting deficiencies are identified?
   - Are periodic reporting procedures, including half-yearly and annual reporting, effective in communicating a balanced and understandable account of the company's position and prospects?

- Are there established channels of communication for individuals to report suspected breaches of laws or regulations or other improprieties?

4. Monitoring
   - Are there ongoing processes embedded within the company's overall business operations, and addressed by senior management, which monitor the effective application of the policies, processes and activities related to internal control and risk management? (Such processes may include control self-assessment, confirmation by personnel of compliance with policies and codes of conduct, internal audit reviews or other management reviews.)
   - Do these processes monitor the company's ability to re-evaluate risks and adjust controls effectively in response to changes in its objectives, its business, and its external environment?
   - Are there effective follow-up procedures to ensure that appropriate change or action occurs in response to changes in risk and control assessments?
   - Is there appropriate communication to the board (or board committees) on the effectiveness of the ongoing monitoring processes on risk and control matters? This should include reporting any significant failings or weaknesses on a timely basis.
   - Are there specific arrangements for management monitoring and reporting to the board on risk and control matters of particular importance? These could include, for example, actual or suspected fraud and other illegal or irregular acts, or matters that could adversely affect the company's reputation or financial position.

The benefits of a good reputation in business

A company's ability to meet the expectations of the important stakeholders associated with it – particularly its customers, business partners, investors, staff and suppliers – has a significant impact on its profitability, its capacity to grow and indeed its overall viability.

This is why reputation has moved out of the public relations arena and into the boardroom. In markets where companies are having to strive harder and harder to secure increasingly scarce resources and more demanding customers, reputation has the potential to be the single differentiating factor between a company and its competitors.

These are some of the views of Michael L Sherman, CEO of AIG Europe, from his chapter in the IoD publication *Reputation Management* (1999). He goes on to say:

Consumers are now more business-literate than in the past, and investors want to see more than just a roll call of healthy tangible assets before they take an equity stake in a company. How stakeholders perceive reputation has become a front-line issue. The business community now accepts that consumers are often reticent about buying products and services from companies with a dubious reputation.

A strong reputation can also serve as an agent for positive change and better performance. More and more companies are using the strength of their corporate reputation in their product marketing and advertising. It is a cohesive umbrella that provides customers with a tacit guarantee about the quality and value of a product. This corporate halo effect is particularly key in markets where it is difficult to differentiate a product or service. When customers are faced with two products or services of equivalent value, the intangible reassurance of a reputable company backing the offer can be the deciding factor.

A company's reputation is important because it affects the way its shareholders and various stakeholders behave towards it. This applies to employees, investors, customers and the general public, and influences such key issues as employee retention, customer satisfaction, customer loyalty and investor relations.

Although it is difficult to pinpoint the exact financial value of a good reputation to a business, the benefits are clear-cut for companies of any size in any sector. A good reputation can:

- *create barriers to competition and inhibit the mobility of rival companies;*
- *attract the best recruits and therefore help avert skill shortages;*
- *attract the best supply chain and business partners;*
- *enhance access to capital and attract investors;*
- *open doors to new markets;*
- *create a premium' value for a company's products and services; and*
- *protect the business in times of crisis.*

As a result of these benefits, reputation is fast becoming the most coveted, if least understood, of all corporate assets for many companies. It is set to play a key role in the way businesses are built in the future. All areas of a business contribute to corporate reputation – it is not just a public relations issue.

For small- and medium-sized companies, a robust reputation makes a difference when competing for capital, employees or customer loyalty. For example, a strong reputation can help smaller private companies when they seek finance for growth or look to divest subsidiaries. All investors – from private individuals to banks to venture capitalists – are influenced by a company's standing in the marketplace. Investors are willing to pay more for equity in companies with a strong reputation than for a stake in less reputable companies which offer otherwise comparable risk and return. The more reputable the company, the lower the risk attached to its capital.

The real value of an equity stake in a private company, or shares in a publicly listed company, is increasingly greater than the total value of its assets. As with brands, an emotional factor often drives values above the financial worth of the investment.

If image is the immediate external perception of an organization, it could be argued that reputation is the historic and cultural dimension of that image – a stakeholder community's 'social memory' of the sum total of a company and its activities. Organizations that are out of step with the attitudes of audiences at a given point in time are unlikely to enjoy a positive reputation. Investing in reputation management is an investment in the future of a company. Historically, good reputations have often been sound indicators of solid financial performance.

Reputation on the line

An event can become a crisis because it threatens a company's short-term prospects and, if the event is mismanaged, its long-term survival. Companies rely on delicate inter-relationships for their mandate to operate. When these relationships are jolted – and profitability threatened – by an internally or externally generated disaster, companies with a strong reputation that act quickly to maintain stakeholder confidence, underpin sales, protect their market position and communicate with regulators will be the companies that go furthest toward guarding shareholder value.

Conversely, companies with dented reputations are likely to find it harder to attract investment, retain customers and employees and compete in chosen markets. A damaged corporate reputation can often be repaired or rebuilt, but ongoing nurturing of reputation can prevent the need for this. Many companies have discovered that a well of goodwill among consumers, the media, suppliers, investors and the community, earned through years of understanding and meeting the needs of all these audiences at different times, can soften the detrimental impact a crisis has on their reputation.

There are two important points about reputation. First, it is a state of mind. It is a set of memories, perceptions and opinions that sits in your stakeholders' consciousness. And second, communicating with your stakeholders should lie at the heart of all your reputation-building activity.

In recent years, the media coverage of business and political issues has grown enormously – so no business can expect to escape unwanted media attention during a crisis. The best defence is not only to be prepared, but also to have built up a substantial bank of goodwill with each stakeholder group over time. This can be powerful enough to secure a second chance for companies even after a catastrophe.

Experienced chairmen expressed the following views on some of the topics covered in this section

Sir Nigel Mobbs

Risk is something all businesses must be involved in – it is essential if one is to get a financial return that is better than gilt-edged securities, that are risk-free. All the judgements that are made on the degree of risk and the measurement of risk rely on professionalism. The board must be aware of the overall risk that the shareholders are likely to be exposed to and ensure the processes are in place to assess risk and report on it. The board should also be satisfied about the competence of the management and ensure that a succession plan is in place. There may well be a succession gap risk at times and in any case, it is a good idea to have an emergency plan too.

Dennis Woods

If anything serious should go wrong or a potential risk emerges I believe that all the directors should know immediately. Generally, we have a 'no surprises' rule and nothing is swept under the carpet. Non-executive directors have the advantage of not being close to the business day to day and so often notice things that could be a risk to the business or else just ask the right questions. Whereas those of us who are there all the time often don't notice things that are right under our noses or take them for granted.

COMPLIANCE AND ETHICS

Leadership and integrity

One of the many roles that a board of directors should fulfil is to give leadership to the organization that it governs. Leadership in this sense includes setting the pace and direction of the organization and also the values and ethos that define its culture – the way people should think and act. This culture becomes manifest most clearly in the statement, 'That's the way we do things around here'. It is probably a fair assumption that most directors in modern society would want their organization's culture to embody integrity as a cornerstone. So, the leadership given by the board should contain a clear message about integrity that is exemplified by the directors' own behaviour.

When considering the question of integrity, directors should have in the forefront of their minds the fact that they owe fiduciary duties to the company on whose board they serve. This means that they are required to act in good faith in the best interests of the company by exercising their powers for the proper purposes for which they were conferred. That requires that they do not place themselves in a position where there is an actual or potential conflict between their duties to the company and their personal interests or duties to third parties. These obligations are met in various ways, in particular:

- Boards should ensure that their company complies with relevant laws, regulations and codes of practice, refrains from any anti-competitive practices, and honours obligations and commitments.
- Individual directors should at all times comply with the law and set an example to help ensure that their company complies with the laws and regulations governing its operations.
- Although not a legal obligation, each director should at all times respect the truth and act honestly in business dealings and in the exercise of all responsibilities as a director.
- Integrity should be the hallmark of each board member's conduct in decision making, uninfluenced by shareholdings, or by business, political or personal commitments and relationships external to his or her company duties.

Most people would be of the view that any legitimate organization should comply with the laws and other regulations that society, through government, has decreed to be pertinent. But is that enough? Should higher and broader standards be considered and, if so, which ones? If this line is followed, to what extent should these standards be influenced by the acid test, 'only if it is good for the company'? And should these considerations be made as part of a broader notion of corporate social responsibility, which takes into account the needs and aspirations of employees, customers, suppliers and society in addition to shareholders? These are questions that every board should consider from time to time in deciding what the company's values and ethical position will be. Perhaps it would be timely to put the topic on your board's agenda shortly.

Ethics and values

In deciding where your organization should fit on the ethical spectrum, your board might first ponder which of the following groupings would be the most apposite. They were identified by Johnson and Scholes (1997), based on some earlier research:

1. Those organizations believing, after Milton Friedman, that the only social responsibility of business is to increase its profit, and that it is government's responsibility to provide through legislation a suitable framework of duties and responsibilities under which business will operate for the common good.
2. Those believing in the above, but who recognize that well-managed relationships with external stakeholders are beneficial, and give rise to the need to monitor behaviour to catch and stop short-term practices of doubtful ethical provenance for the sake of the long-term business benefit.
3. Those believing that stakeholder interests need more explicit incorporation in the objectives of the business, and that performance means more than just the bottom line. For instance, retaining uneconomic jobs in deprived areas, or not trading in products perceived as harmful, though a balance clearly needs to be maintained to preserve the long-term health of the business.
4. Those founded in response to a community need, where financial considerations are secondary to society's needs, and the balance is usually so weighted that finance becomes simply a constraint on providing primarily for the interests of the beneficiary as the most important stakeholder.

An increasing number of companies take the view that high ethical standards are no longer a luxury but a necessity. They see them as a source of competitive advantage, a way of protecting their reputation and attracting and keeping customers and good staff, a way of being the sort of company that people respect and trust, thus underpinning the business. This approach considers good corporate citizenship as making good business sense, so that everyone wins.

Whatever position your board decides is appropriate for your organization in future, it makes sense to prepare a statement of what ethical policies are intended. Even if your ethical position will be unaltered, it is still good practice to have it in writing for all to see. It can be a helpful guide to staff in day-to-day decisions, can be used as part of the induction process for new employees, and to make customers, suppliers and others aware of the integrity of your organization and its ethical stance.

The process of drawing up such a code will help your directors to reflect on how the organization operates in relation to its various stakeholders and how the values it considers important can be maintained. Such statements are variously called: Statement on / Policies on / Code of – Conduct / Ethics / Business Ethics / Principles / Values / Philosophy. You may find it helpful to obtain a copy of the checklist and illustrative code published by the Institute of Business Ethics (Webley, 1998). It recommends that the following areas be considered when drawing up such a document:

- General principles to be adopted.
- Relations with customers.
- Relations with shareholders.
- Relations with employees.
- Relations with suppliers.
- Relations with government and the local communities.
- Relations with competitors.
- Issues relating to international business.
- Behaviour during mergers and takeovers.
- Compliance and verification.

Experienced chairmen expressed the following views on some of the topics covered in this section

Sir Nigel Mobbs

On the matters of compliance and ethics, I see the main role of the chairman to ensure that the company's culture is such that it is compatible with the industry norm, but at a high level – without being in an ivory tower. Compliance starts at the top. The board must decide on an appropriate code of ethics and make sure it is written out for all employees.

Linda Smith

We have spent quite a lot of time looking at ethics and have held various seminars on the subject over the last couple of years for us and clinicians from all the major trusts. We put them on, not to look at making any hard and fast decisions but to get the proper body of the health service locally thinking and sharing with each other. One thing that did come up in particular was that it was recognized that it's really very important that clinicians can understand what sort of consensus there is around some of these issues. They should be able to talk with other people, should be able to have some constructive thinking and challenge to their own thinking. The board took part in this setting up process, which was very important, but we opened it up to a wider group of people.

ACCOUNTABILITY AND RESPONSIBILITY

Directors are often unclear about exactly who they are accountable and responsible to, and for what. For example, can they be accountable to more than one 'master'? To what extent are they responsible *for* the actions of the employees and for meeting customer needs? Do they have responsibilities *to* employees, customers and suppliers, and if so to what degree?

The way in which companies are legally incorporated makes clear that the duties of the board are owed to the company, so the wellbeing of the organization must be the first responsibility of its directors. However, in considering the interests of the company, the directors are jointly and severally accountable to the shareholders as a whole for its stewardship and for meeting their appropriate interests. The board also has responsibility to meet the appropriate interests of the company's stakeholders. In this context, stakeholders can be defined as 'individuals or groups, apart from shareholders, whom the board judges on occasion to have an appropriate interest in, and/or influence over, the company's operations and the achievement of the company's goals' (*Standards for the Board*, IoD, 2001). One would expect such appropriate interests to embrace being treated in an honest and fair manner at all times but not to meet their every demand or whim. It is for every board to judge what it sees as appropriate in each case and to lay down policies for general guidance.

Beyond this, various Acts of Parliament have imposed wider responsibilities on companies and their directors. These require them to evaluate their actions in a broad social context and oblige them to consider the impact of their business on others. In particular, attention needs to be paid to the protection of the physical environment, matters of employee occupational health and safety, employee relations including equal opportunities, working hours and minimum wages, rules on consumer protection and competition rules. There are additional laws and regulations that affect specific areas of business, such as financial services, healthcare and public utilities. The Companies Act also makes explicit provision for directors to recognize the interests of employees. In addition, there are laws that apply to contracts entered into by the company with third parties.

In this way, directors and the companies for which they are responsible are held answerable to society through legislation, which is distinct from the directors' accountability to the shareholders (or whatever other body might occupy a similar position in relation to the board and the organization concerned). In mutual societies the shareholders are also the customers, and a similar relationship exists in organizations like trusts in the National Health Service, where the patients are those for whose benefit the organization primarily exists and for whom it was originally created.

So, whatever the organization, the board of directors (sometimes called something else, such as a council) has principal accountability to those for whom the entity primarily exists (eg, the shareholders). But it is also answerable to society through the laws and regulations by which directors and those for whose actions they are ultimately responsible, principally employees, should comply. The final sanctions on directors are dismissal by the shareholders and action through the courts and tribunals, resulting in fines, disqualification, stigma or imprisonment.

Many boards face dilemmas when they make judgements that attempt to reconcile their responsibilities to those to whom they are accountable, their responsibilities to stakeholders and their fiduciary duty to act in the best interests of the company. The power of dismissal that shareholders collectively have over the directors can sometimes create conflicts and tensions that blunt the sharp balance of those judgements. This can often be the biggest dilemma facing directors. It is most obviously apparent to directors of subsidiary companies and many private companies where one or two of the directors are also powerful shareholders. In such circumstances, there can also sometimes be potential conflict when matters of probity and accountability for public money are involved.

As chairman of the board, you have a special obligation to remind your colleagues of their various responsibilities whenever these apparent conflicts have to be reconciled and to guide their consequent deliberations with particular skill.

Experienced chairmen expressed the following views on some of the topics covered in this section

Sir Nigel Mobbs

I strongly believe that the board is accountable only to the company's shareholders, while also being held to account by society through the legal and regulatory framework. The board has a responsibility to others, such as employees, creditors and customers. There is a plethora of legislation that companies have a responsibility to observe in this area and in some cases there is an element of conflict between them that must be judged.

Linda Smith

The third area is accountability; accountability up to ministers for the implementation of the general spirit of government policy and making decisions around that – prioritizing, knowing what is important for our area. Then there is accountability to the wider population and balancing those two things is tricky and the proper role of the board is to get that into balance – to know what it means to balance those two areas of accountability.

A thing that we do which is maybe different from boards in the private sector is that we make our decisions, by and large, in public. Members of the public do come when there is a decision to make about an issue that may be controversial. Members of the local Community Health Councils certainly come to our meetings and are avid watchers of what we do, and I welcome that. They are a second string in keeping us accountable – our accountability is there in the room with us in part and I invite them to speak on topics where they have indicated they have something to say, as I do with members of the public. I make it clear that they cannot enter into discussion with us but it can be useful to hear their point of view.

COMMUNICATIONS AND RELATIONSHIP MANAGEMENT

Determining and reviewing communications policies

Deciding communications policy is not something that the board can sensibly delegate. Companies that do not review their corporate communications at board level are taking a risk. In his book *Managing Your Reputation*, Haywood (1994) explains how the board can deal with the establishment and review of communications policy:

> *Of course, many directors will protest that too much is being squeezed on to overcrowded agendas. Yet with proper planning, the review of a responsibly run programme takes little time. Indeed, the fact that the board signs off the*

company's communications/PR policy at least annually will help to ensure that the programme is run responsibly.

The chairman or chief executive must take the final responsibility for the effectiveness of company communications and public relations. Every member of the board owes it to the chairman to share that responsibility and to ensure that the necessary information is available to allow intelligent discussion of key communications issues at board meetings. Where the company is not advised by an independent public relations professional, the need for board reviews becomes even more important. The board should be concerned that:

- the communications policy is sound;
- all who have a right to know are properly informed;
- effective feedback systems exist;
- early warning of problems can be assured;
- the processes exist to deal briskly and sensitively with any crisis;
- a public relations strategy is in place;
- a specific director is personally responsible for public relations with proper, regular reporting procedures to the whole board.

The only satisfactory reporting method must be for communications to be a regular and routine *board item. It will not be necessary for the board to become involved in the detail, but each director must be comfortable that he or she has a good overview. Directors should not just be concerning themselves with communications when there is a problem. When problems strike, it may be too late to apply remedial treatment. Effective relations between the organization and its various audiences require constant attention.*

Public relations strategy might be reviewed once or twice a year and a strategy review paper presented to the board could cover the following areas:

1. *Objectives.* What is to be achieved over the coming period to support the corporate objectives? Aims for the communications efforts may be acceptable, but could these be quantified to identify specific points that should be reached over agreed periods of time?
2. *Strategy.* What *tone of voice* is being adopted to achieve these objectives? Do all the elements support this and

how do they combine into an overall plan? Is each activity complementary? Can any be extended to reach broader audiences and improve cost-effectiveness?

3. *Perceptions.* How is the company seen? What are the attitudes of those whose goodwill we need for success? (Periodically these must be identified by research, but interim reviews should note the observations of public relations, marketing, sales, personnel and other professionals in contact with prime audiences.)
4. *Messages.* How do we *wish* the company to be seen? Have we properly identified all the audiences we wish to influence? What gaps are there between reality and perception? Is the company communicating in the way that will win support – and *behaving* in the way that will win support? Are all the communications activities reinforcing these agreed messages?
5. *Tactics.* What communications methods are to be used? How will these relate to other corporate activities? Who is directing and implementing the programme? What company contingency plans have been proposed to deal with the unexpected?
6. *Initiatives.* Are there special events of which we should be aware? Where they relate to strategic matters, how can they best be tied in to the broader company business timetable?
7. *Calendar.* What are the major activities in the corporate calendar that have public relations implications? What are the plans to support these? Is the programme scheduled realistically to coordinate such events with any new communications initiatives?
8. *Concerns.* What issues might the communications professionals wish to discuss? Are there areas of policy where the directors' views and support are essential? Will members of the board be expected to participate functionally? If not, might these be enhanced if they did?
9. *Competition.* Are there public relations activities by competitors that should be discussed? How is their public

relations effectiveness, say, in the tone of media coverage, compared with yours? Is this competitive position improving?

10. *Appraisal.* How effective is the programme overall? What performance criteria are set so that the effectiveness can be appraised and the direction fine tuned? What are the achievements to date, ideally measured against the objectives that were set?

11. *Management.* How is the competence of those charged with managing the function? Do directors have any commendations or concerns that should be voiced? How are consultants or other advisers performing? Are there any changes that need to be considered?

12. *Resources.* What is the total cost of the activity proposed, including staff time? Does anything require additional company resources, such as regional seminars, factory open days, dealer or wholesaler briefings? How well prepared and resourced is the communications team to handle any crisis that may arise?

Promoting goodwill

Many chairmen take on the responsibility of personally liaising with shareholders and one or a number of stakeholders and building good personal relationships with key individuals. In addition to these specific responsibilities, a great deal of goodwill can be created if the chairman takes the time and trouble to speak with the company's staff frequently, informally and sincerely.

It is clear that adopting a proactive approach to communicating with shareholders and relevant stakeholders can be the best way to help safeguard the reputation of the organization. Indeed, this is the most apposite means of achieving their support and goodwill, which can be crucial in times of crisis. Such an approach requires the board to be collectively committed to *promoting and enhancing* the goodwill of the parties concerned, with clear responsibilities agreed for liaising with each of them. It is crucial that proper procedures are established for managing relationships with these audiences both day to day and at times of crisis.

Waiting for a crisis to occur before finding out if these procedures and responsibilities are adequate is imprudent, to say the least. Rather, they should be stringently tested periodically, with a report being submitted to the board. A full range of possible eventualities should be considered, covering the shareholders and all the relevant stakeholder groups.

From time to time you could encourage the directors to review the identity of relevant stakeholders and have an unfettered discussion on what crisis eventualities might be taken into account. This could be done on the same occasions that communications and risk policies are being considered by the board.

Experienced chairmen expressed the following views on some of the topics covered in this section

Sir Nigel Mobbs

The promotion of goodwill is very important because it can have a tangible benefit to the company in terms of image and performance. Generally speaking, companies that communicate well tend to perform better because such a culture brings with it a sense of pride to all employees that things are evident. It is helpful for companies to be transparent and to communicate well with employees, customers and the local community where appropriate. It is usually best to tell them what you are doing rather than ask if you should, but if you were considering something that might be controversial, then consultation would be appropriate.

Linda Smith

The government has decreed that there shall be a non-executive director from the Health Authority on every Primary Care Group board and since there are six of them in this area we are very hard pressed. We have set up a system here where my chief executive and I meet all the Primary Care Group chairs together, so that in a sense we carry out joint responsibility, but they are formally accountable to him. The non-executive director on the PCG board is not a representative but is trying to make sure that the links are there and the communication channels are freed up. They should be helping the PCG board to develop and to be aware of the wider picture and Health Authority perspective. The directors from my board have also been important in terms of speaking about how a board should operate, from their experience here.

Communications and relationship management are very important for us. I don't think we've got communications upward and outward right, nor communications within the health service right, but we are working on it. At the moment, we do have to be particularly aware of changing public perceptions, expectations and demands of the health service. I think we have to be much better at communicating openly and transparently. There is a sea change nationally in the way people are thinking and feeling about this now.

Another thing I probably should say about what I have tried to do personally in my own role is to recognize the importance of building relationships more widely, which I think is a key role of the chair. This involves being part of things external to the organization so that you can provide enough influence upward when you need to. The trick is not to take on too much so that you can't spend enough time on the job; there has to be a balance, but it is important not to just get your head down here. We are very visible, for a host of reasons, so it is very important to be able to get to people who have influence and to build those networks. I am a great believer in building good personal relationships so that it's easier to handle the difficult times.

CHAPTER CHECKLIST

Here are some questions you might ask yourself in connection with the matters covered in this chapter before you plan any consequent action:

- Is your board averse to taking risks such that the company could fall behind its competitors?

- Is your board's disposition towards risk appropriate to present circumstances?
- ... and if not, have you planned for a discussion to agree a change of approach?
- How sure is your board that risks to the company are minimized by the proper management and control of risk?
- ... and if there is doubt, have the questions on pages 67 to 69 under the headings of *risk assessment, control environment and control activities, information and communication* and *monitoring* been addressed?
- ... and do the directors use their collective judgement to assess the degree and importance of each area of risk to identify where most effort should be made?
- Does your board fully recognize the range of benefits to your company of a good business reputation?
- ... and is it promoting policies that will provide ongoing nurturing of that reputation on a broad front?
- Do all your directors fully understand their fiduciary duties to the company?
- ... and do they consistently comply with laws and regulations and behave with integrity and honesty?
- Does your board endeavour to ensure that the company complies with relevant laws, regulations and codes of practice?
- Has your board recently considered what the organization's ethical position and values should be and whether company policies in this area need clarifying and updating?
- Does a written statement of the company's ethical position that is widely available, understood and upheld, underpin such policies?
- When your board is faced with the need to reconcile conflicting responsibilities and obligations, do you guide the deliberations with particular skill?
- Does your board decide communications policy?
- ... and take final responsibility for its effective implementation, with regular, comprehensive reviews?

- Is there a specific director accountable to the board for public relations matters?
- Is a public relations strategy in place, addressing the questions posed on pages 80 to 82?
- Are procedures established for managing relationships with shareholders and all relevant stakeholders?
- ... and are they stringently tested periodically, with a report to the board?
- Do the directors periodically consider what crisis eventualities might be taken into account in relation to various third parties?

5

Board composition

ATTRIBUTES NEEDED AROUND THE BOARD TABLE

Looking ahead

The composition of each board is unique, not only because the combination of individuals is usually peculiar to a particular board but because the business of each board is different, calling upon a distinct mix of characteristics from the board members. What mix might be appropriate for your board and how can you assess what might be the best composition in future? Remember that the board you have now has been responsible for the past decisions. In this regard the directors may have done well, or maybe they should have performed their tasks better. In any event, you should consider what the future may hold over the next few years and decide what changes to the board might be needed to ensure the continuing success and prosperity of the organization. After all, the measure of your success as chairman is the assembly of directors that sit around your board table. If they are likely to be inadequate for the challenges that lie ahead, *you* will fail. As their leader you should do something about it.

Perhaps the first consideration should centre on examining the variety and complexity of the issues that your board will need to address. To do this you must try to look ahead from a strategic perspective and also assess the likely regimes in the regulatory and ethical environments for your organization. Consider the attitude to commercial risk that might be needed too, and if your board's present disposition would be appropriate. Remember that essentially the board is there to make the important decisions that will determine the ongoing success and prosperity of the organization. At the same time, it should provide pertinent leadership, guidance and advice. So, above all, you should contemplate the decision making and leadership capabilities that will be needed in the months and years immediately ahead and compare them with the current situation.

Think about the 'conditioning' tasks the board will have to consider and whether the current board possesses the required depth of experience and personal attributes to address them comprehensively:

- Will the board embrace the need for change and be visionary enough to set a fitting direction and pace for the company, with an appropriate balance of risk and potential reward?
- How well will the board judge the inevitable future dilemmas that it will face?
- Will the board be able to consider and agree policies that will be appropriate for the company's future needs in such areas as standards of behaviour, shareholder and stakeholder communications, compliance, employment and customer relations?
- Will corporate governance issues be addressed with relevant expertise and competence?

Consider the complexity and scale of the 'enterprise' tasks that the board is likely to face and the issues to be dealt with. Then ask yourself if the present directors will be able to understand and judge them sufficiently to ensure that proper advantage is taken of the opportunities:

- Will the proper weightings be made between the long and short term?
- Will the right business ventures be pursued?
- Will the necessary major commitments in the areas of finance, people, market development, product/service development, and physical resources be made?

- Will suitable alliances be sought?
- Will the board possess the necessary skills and knowledge competently to oversee management's execution of agreed objectives and plans?
- What advice could the board give regarding the calibre of senior staff?
- Will the company's prosperity be assured?

In many organizations there is a real or perceived degree of prescription about the makeup of the board. However, you should resist accepting directors that are nominated to represent the interests of significant shareholders or other interest groups, unless you can have a say in who they are. Such nominations are often made by venture capitalists and are usually a feature of joint venture companies. They are also frequently found in mutual or cooperative organizations and in the public sector, the National Health Service being an example.

While one must usually accept that nominees are a condition of the makeup of such boards, it does not necessarily mean that the chairman can have no say in the selection of the individuals appointed. Indeed, concern for the ongoing wellbeing of the organization must override any sectional interests, so that the capability of the board becomes paramount. That capability will owe as much to the balance of the board and the dynamic cohesion of the directors as to the proficiency of any one individual. It is therefore crucial that more than one nominee candidate is presented, from which the most appropriate person can be selected.

Personal characteristics

Let us consider the personal characteristics that you will be expecting members of your board to exhibit, some of which you will be looking for in new appointees. The point here is that while one director will have strengths in some areas and weaknesses in others, another may possess complementary qualities. By considering which particular characteristics are deficient in your board, bearing in mind the strengths and weaknesses of existing directors, you will know just which ones to prefer in any new recruit to help in building a more effective working group.

The directors' personal characteristics that I suggest you consider first are those identified in research instigated by the IoD and listed in their publication *Standards for the Board* (2001). The 35 individual personal attributes described were found to be those regarded as important for effective boards of directors to exhibit. It is most unlikely that any one director will have all the personal attributes that are listed. They are clustered into six groups under appropriate headings, which you will probably find easier to use in identifying where your board may need strengthening, once you understand the individual attributes that apply to each group. The group headings are:

1. decision making;
2. communication;
3. interaction with others;
4. analysis and the use of information;
5. strategic perception;
6. achievement of results (business competence).

The full list of attributes under each heading is shown below.

In addition, I recommend that you consider which of the following personal qualities might be desirable in a new appointee:

7. courage/strength of character;
8. common sense;
9. perseverance;
10. diplomacy/tact;
11. wisdom;
12. intellect.

Directors' personal attributes

1. Decision making

- *Critical faculty:* Probes the facts, challenges assumptions, identifies the (dis)advantages of proposals, provides counter arguments, ensures discussions are penetrating.

- *Decisiveness:* Shows a readiness to take decisions and take action. Is able to make up his or her mind.
- *Judgement:* Makes sensible decisions or recommendations by weighing evidence. Considers reasonable assumptions, the ethical dimension and factual information.

2. Communication

- *Listening skills:* Listens dispassionately, intently and carefully so that key points are recalled and taken into account, questioning when necessary to ensure understanding.
- *Openness:* Is frank and open when communicating. Willing to admit errors and shortcomings.
- *Presentation skills:* Conveys ideas, images and words in a way that shows empathy with the audience.
- *Responsiveness:* Is able to invite and accept feedback.
- *Verbal fluency:* Speaks clearly, audibly and has good diction. Is concise, avoids jargon and tailors content to the audience's needs.
- *Written communication skills:* Written matter is readily intelligible; ideas, information and opinions are conveyed accurately, clearly and concisely.

3. Interaction with others

- *Confidence:* Is aware of own strengths and weaknesses. Is assured when dealing with others. Able to take charge of a situation when appropriate.
- *Coordination skills:* Adopts appropriate interpersonal styles and methods in guiding the board towards task accomplishment. Fosters cooperation and effective teamwork.
- *Flexibility:* Adopts a flexible (but not compliant) style when interacting with others. Takes their views into account and changes position when appropriate.
- *Integrity:* Is truthful and trustworthy and can be relied upon to keep his or her word. Does not have double standards and does not compromise on ethical and legal matters.

- *Learning ability:* Seeks and acquires new knowledge and skills from multiple sources, including board experience.
- *Motivation:* Inspires others to achieve goals by ensuring a clear understanding of what needs to be achieved and by showing commitment, enthusiasm, encouragement and support.
- *Persuasiveness:* Persuades others to give their agreement and commitment; in face of conflict, uses personal influence to achieve consensus and / or agreement.
- *Presence:* Makes a strong positive impression on first meeting. Has authority and credibility, establishes rapport quickly.
- *Sensitivity:* Shows an understanding of the feelings and needs of others, and a willingness to provide personal support or to take other actions as appropriate.

4. Analysis and the use of information

- *Consciousness of detail:* Insists that sufficiently detailed and reliable information be taken account of and reported as necessary.
- *Eclecticism:* Systematically seeks all possible relevant information from a variety of sources.
- *Numeracy:* Assimilates numerical and statistical information accurately, understands its derivation and makes sensible, sound interpretations.
- *Problem recognition:* Identifies problems and identifies possible or actual causes.

5. Strategic perception

- *Change-orientation:* Alert and responsive to the need for change. Encourages new initiatives and the implementation of new policies, structures and practices.
- *Creativity:* Generates and recognizes imaginative solutions and innovations.
- *Foresight:* Is able to imagine possible future states and characteristics of the company in a future environment.

- *Organizational awareness:* Is aware of the company's strengths and weaknesses and of the likely impact of the board's decisions upon them.
- *Perspective:* Rises above the immediate problem or situation and sees the wider issues and implications. Is able to relate disparate facts and see all relevant relationships.
- *Strategic awareness:* Is aware of the various factors that determine the company's opportunities and threats (for example, shareholder, stakeholder, market, technological, environmental and regulatory factors).

6. Achievement of results (business competence)

- *Business acumen:* Has the ability to identify opportunities to increase the company's business advantage.
- *Delegation skills:* Distinguishes between what should be done by others or by him- or herself. Allocates decision making or other tasks to appropriate colleagues and subordinates.
- *Drive:* Shows energy, vitality and commitment.
- *Exemplar:* Sets challenging but achievable goals and standards of performance for self and others.
- *Resilience:* Maintains composure and effectiveness in the face of adversity, setbacks, opposition or unfairness.
- *Risk acceptance:* Is prepared to take action that involves calculated risk in order to achieve a desired benefit or advantage.
- *Tenacity:* Stays with a position or plan of action until the desired objectives are achieved or require adaptation.

Knowledge and experience

In addition to considering these personal characteristics, you will need to examine what knowledge and experience will be needed and identify where the shortages are. In doing this it may be useful to recognize a) any special knowledge and experience that would be useful or even necessary on your board, b) the general knowledge that all directors should have, and c) specific roles that must be played well.

Special knowledge and experience

A really well-balanced board will have directors with a variety of experience from different backgrounds and professional disciplines. This variety helps to create the positive dynamic and span of capability that characterize a board which is really competent at addressing *the full range* of its tasks. Such a board will be capable of looking at each topic from several aspects at once in intrinsically different ways. Compare this with a board made up of people who are largely from the same discipline, industry or job experience – they will probably all get along very well together but are more likely to miss opportunities and make mistakes. This is where the choice of non-executive directors with particular knowledge and experience can make a crucial difference to a board's balance and capability.

General knowledge and experience

Despite the specific areas of functional management responsibility that executive directors may have, all directors should acquire a universal attitude to the board's affairs. That is not to say that they will not be particularly well informed in their areas of specialization and bring this knowledge to bear on the board's deliberations. Indeed, the balance of the board will be strengthened by having a diversity of specialist knowledge to call upon, from both executive and non-executive directors. But a board comprised of people who are seen only as specialists and whose observations and comments are restricted to their limited areas of expertise will be severely compromised in its decision making capacity. The directors on a board need to speak and understand a common language, see the enterprise as a whole and appreciate how its various functional elements interrelate. In short, regardless of any specialist knowledge they may have, all directors should endeavour to think and act as generalists and you must encourage them to do so.

It will help greatly if each director has acquired cognizance of at least what is regarded as the minimum set of *knowledge* and techniques required by a company director. The Institute of Directors has defined this minimum set, which is covered in its

Company Direction Programme of courses for directors. It comprises the following areas, with which directors should be familiar:

- *The role of company director and the board.* The crucial differences between direction, ownership and management. Corporate governance issues. The board's purpose, tasks, functions, structure and mode of effective operation.
- *The director and the law.* The legal framework that directors operate in, with an in-depth understanding of their legal responsibilities.
- *Strategic business direction.* The issues and processes involved in formulating, implementing and controlling the company's corporate and business strategies.
- *Finance for non-financial directors.* Basic knowledge of accounting, financial language and concepts, and the use of relevant financial tools and techniques to evaluate and monitor business financial health. The compilation of statutory financial statements and reports. The relative merits of various sources of company finance.
- *Human resource direction.* The importance of employing the right people with the right skills and encouraging and developing their commitment, involvement and contribution. The alignment of HR strategy, policies and practices with corporate strategy. The implications of employment law.
- *Effective marketing strategies.* The vital role of successful marketing strategies in creating customer value and improving a company's market performance and how they should be devised, implemented and controlled.
- *Leadership and strategic change.* The board's leadership role in accomplishing change and anticipating and overcoming resistance to it. Defining the external and internal pressures for change within the company and the processes for implementing change.

The more general *experience* that directors can bring to the board table will principally comprise experience of business, management and board practice. Here, variety as well as depth of experience will enrich the board. A board that is dominated by people whose experience has been largely limited to one industry, or even to one company or one board of directors, will clearly benefit from the wider views provided by colleagues with richer and more varied experiences.

While relevant knowledge in itself is necessary to the board's work, experience enhances the understanding, analysis and application of that knowledge. This enhancement can be particularly valuable with regard to business knowledge and knowledge of board practice. Here again, well selected non-executive directors can usually enhance the board in these areas.

Roles to be played

The various roles that a director might fulfil can be usefully looked at by considering the broad areas to which they relate. These areas are 1) external to the company, 2) within the company, and 3) within the board. The 12 roles are characterized as follows under those headings:

1. *External to the company*
   A. Know How: Providing relevant expertise and knowledge.
   B. Know What: Providing facts and information.
   C. Know Who: Having useful personal contacts.
   D. Influencer: Being influential because of reputation and standing or having the ability to influence other people or organizations.
2. *Within the company*
   E. Know How: Providing relevant expertise and knowledge.
   F. Know What: Providing facts and information.
   G. Know Who: Knowing the key people and their strengths and weaknesses.
   H. Ambassador: Displaying exemplary advocacy of the board, behaving with integrity, consistency and fairness.
3. *Within the board*
   I. Supportive: Being a counsellor, adviser, supporter and listener.
   J. Creative: Solving problems, generating ideas and recognizing opportunities.
   K. Political: Challenging, influencing, encouraging and being decisive.
   L. Overseeing: Observing, probing, questioning and monitoring.

Each director should be able to play a number of these roles well. If you recognize any role that none or few of your board members can play well, it may identify an area that could be strengthened. In some areas this can be achieved by application over time, but more often one will be seeking these strengths in new appointees.

Experienced chairmen expressed the following views on some of the topics covered in this section

Sir Nigel Mobbs

Looking at the attributes needed, you must get a broad balance of experience and not only experience of the company's business. I think the spread could include people with experience from other business sectors and from a public service background too. There needs to be a balance of specialist skills as well. I don't favour former consultants used by the firm or other professionals such as solicitors – you can buy their services when needed.

Linda Smith

When considering board composition we must think about attributes and the board as a team, as well as just the specific experience elements of it. I think you need people who can contribute with their personal characteristics as well, in terms of participating.

GETTING THE BALANCE RIGHT

It is not easy to achieve a well-balanced board of directors. Indeed, it could be argued that there is really no such thing as a completely balanced board, since the notion of balance can apply to a number of different areas. Nevertheless, it is well worth trying to attain a high degree of balance in as many areas as you can. The main general areas where balance can be attempted are:

- personal characteristics;
- special knowledge and experience;
- executive directors/non-executive directors;
- directors' roles.

Personal characteristics

When considering personal characteristics, you will also need to be mindful of the personality of anyone who might join in relation to the 'personality' and style of your board. Will new people fit in and complement the board's style or should it be changed anyway, in which case how could new recruits help? Remember that the more effective boards have a style with a degree of dynamic tension that creates healthy discussion. Would the inclusion of some people in a particular age group help here? Should the gender balance of your board be changed? You may have some 'sleepers', directors with narrow perceptions, and 'nodding donkeys' filling valuable spaces around your board table. They merit being developed or replaced with more able people to create a well-balanced top team that is of high calibre and competence.

Special knowledge and experience

When it comes to considering the balance of special knowledge and experience that will be appropriate for your board, you are probably the best judge. Each situation is unique and is conditioned by the type of business activity the organization is engaged in. The only sensible general guidance is to try to avoid having too many directors with the same specialist background. Aim at achieving a good balance of people from a variety of appropriate experience backgrounds and professional disciplines. Also consider whether the profile of board experience needs to be enhanced. While it is important to take experience into account, remember that in many areas of business today it can be dangerous to place too much reliance on past experience. Therefore, a balance must be struck between experience and an attitude of unlearning and relearning.

Executive and non-executive directors

There are many differing opinions regarding the best balance of executive and non-executive directors for optimum board effectiveness. In some industry sectors such as insurance, building societies and banks, boards are often constituted with a preponderance of non-executive directors. This is also the case in many of the larger listed companies in the UK and in most listed companies of any size in the United States. For UK listed companies, the *Combined Code on Corporate Governance* requires that, 'At least half the board, excluding the chairman, should comprise non-executive directors determined by the board to be independent. A smaller company should have at least two.' The boards of organizations in the not-for-profit sector will often be predominantly non-executive. Most private companies and, indeed, small companies generally, will have boards that are either comprised exclusively of executive directors or have a majority of them.

This wide variety of approaches obscures the fact that a proper balance of executive and non-executive directors can optimize the benefits of the unitary board system. This system essentially balances the energetic pragmatism and hands-on knowledge of the executives with the breadth of experience, reflective wisdom and perception of the non-executive directors. However, prescription on this matter in the Articles of Association, or a similar incorporating document may, in some cases, limit your ability to make the changes that you feel would provide a better balance to your board in this respect. If such restrictions do not apply, and the only ones seem to be custom and practice, why not consider making the changes that will create a better, more effective board? If they do apply, seek to change them if you can.

Directors' roles

To help you to properly identify the strengths and weaknesses of your board in terms of both the directors' personal characteristics and the roles that they can play, you can utilize the diagnostic chart shown in Figure 5.1, later in this chapter. It will enable you to see at a glance where the gaps are and where your board is 'overweight', once you have filled it in.

Experienced chairmen expressed the following views on some of the topics covered in this section

Michael Mander

I think it is very advantageous to have one non-executive director who is a master of detail – even a nitpicker, although I wouldn't like him or her to identify themselves as such. One should also aim to get multiple benefits from each appointment. One of the non-executive directors on my board is both a UK and a US lawyer, which is a very useful combination for a UK company that does a lot of business in the United States. He is also a non-executive director of other companies operating in several countries, so he brings worldwide experience and legal knowledge.

Dennis Woods

Looking at the makeup of the board, it is good to have directors who are a bit cautious, as a counter to me and my brother, who tend to be go-getting. This creates an environment for compromise, where some are trying to pull on the reins while we are trying to charge forward – so we tend to take more of a middle of the road path in the end. If I can't properly answer questions of caution then we shouldn't be doing it, at least not without a deeper look. This tension makes for a nice balance of the board, which is what is needed. All in all it is important to get people with the potential to be good directors and recognize that they need development.

Sir Nigel Mobbs

As far as obtaining a good board balance is concerned, I think that the ratio of executive to non-executive directors should be about 50:50 for a quoted company. Even private companies should have boards with no less than one-third of the directors being non-executive. However, there should always be more than one non-executive director on a board. Being a sole non-executive on a board with, say, five executive directors is a pretty invidious position – there must be critical mass.

Linda Smith

Society, if you like, is changing in its expectations. It's very important for us, in that regard, that we have a board that can take a wider perspective, because the health service can be very inward looking and it particularly affects issues around having such a large and important professional workforce. The health service has a very strong professional body that, historically, is used to making decisions towards patients – and the world is changing. Therefore, I have on my board a very senior person, who is also a lawyer from local government, who understands what's happening in the world of local government and how they approach issues of governance and accountability. I have people who have been active in the community; a senior university appointee, who is also a very senior clinician and understands the world of medical education; someone from industry who has also been a lay member of a PCG; and someone who is director of personnel of the National Lottery charity board. For me, these people bring a challenge, another perspective and another world to our deliberations. They are often wondering why it is that something is so difficult, why it is that we do things in a particular way. It is really quite important to make people think again. The executive directors welcome this, because we have very good relationships, but they are challenging.

BOARD SIZE AND STRUCTURE

Board size

There are many factors that influence the size of a board. The number and profile of directors will be influenced by such factors as the size, history, ownership, structure and complexity of the company. Sometimes the maximum and/or minimum number of directors is stipulated, usually in the Articles of Association. In other cases an historic merger created a composite board whose structure or size seem now to be immutable. The boards of some smaller companies seem to be structured around the number of important executive functions in the company, each of which seem to deserve a director on the board. Industry sector norms are often thought to be a deciding factor – 'What would be implied if our board's size was halved?' Some organizations, usually with over-large boards, have a number of board members purporting to represent the interests and views of various external parties, that have become enshrined by custom and practice rather than current or future relevance. Most of these apparent restrictions can be overcome, if there is a desire and a will to do so.

The overriding factor determining the board's size should be the need for well-informed decision making. Since this is the primary consideration, an effective board should usually have 4 to 10 members – 12 maximum. Surveys conducted on board size for

UK companies indicate that they typically comprise six or seven directors. Companies listed on the stock exchange have somewhat larger than average boards (typically seven or eight directors), with the boards of the top few hundred companies being rather larger.

Boards become relatively more difficult for the chairman to lead and manage as the numbers increase above 10 directors. The opportunity for any individual on such boards to make an impact on the decision making is more limited and the meetings can easily become 'talking shops'. Cabals and factions tend to form in large boards, which can stifle or overwhelm open discussion and exploration. Indeed, the unwieldy nature and poor dynamics of such boards force many of their chairmen to resort to discussions with small groups of the directors outside the boardroom to 'fix' important decisions prior to the meeting. These larger boards often behave more like committees than the well-informed group of responsible professionals needed to make the all-important insights and decisions at the head of a company or similar organization.

Below the lower end of the preferred range, the group is likely to be dominated by the views and personality of one person. In any case, it is unlikely that two or three people would have the spread of knowledge, experience, perception and acumen to adequately inform the range of issues faced by a board of even the most straightforward of organizations. Indeed, the complexity and scope of topics that most boards face will alone require that there be more than four directors for adequate effectiveness.

Board structure

Our principal concern here is with variants of the unitary board structure that is common in companies and many other organizations in the UK and elsewhere. This structure has as its essence the inclusion of individuals who are in the employ of the company in an executive or management capacity. While the boards of smaller companies are frequently comprised entirely of executive directors, the inclusion of some non-executive directors is quite customary as companies grow. However, some organizations, including a few companies, have a governing body that does not include people who are active in the management of the entity. Such a body is described as a non-executive or supervisory board, or council.

One of the primary strengths of the unitary board is that it can be simultaneously informed and influenced by both the executive and non-executive directors. Its decisions are thus taken with all directors potentially sharing the same information and being aware of each other's opinions and concerns. Thus, the executive directors enact the board's decisions while being fully aware of the attitudes and opinions of their colleagues and how the non-executives' views have been taken into account. To benefit fully from these potential dynamics, many experienced chairmen feel that the contingent of non-executive directors should make up between a quarter and a half of the board, with a minimum of two non-executive directors.

While the all-executive board is quite common in private companies, particularly smaller ones, it is also the norm in companies that are subsidiaries of larger companies or groups. Some of these companies with all-executive boards are of substantial size and complexity and would clearly benefit from the inclusion of some well-chosen non-executive directors. The decision for not doing so is frequently made by a prominent, usually dominant shareholder (such as the holding company), who precludes such an idea.

Some of the more enlightened groups either require the appointment of 'independent' external non-executive directors to the boards of their subsidiaries or encourage internal appointments. These internal non-executive appointments allow an executive director from one subsidiary to sit on the board of another within the group. These cross-directorships enrich the perception and decision making of the boards, help to encourage their focus on proper board issues and act as an effective personal development tool for those taking part in a non-executive capacity.

The structure of the boards of many smaller companies (and some larger ones) is built around the functional responsibilities of the executive directors. This usually stems from the makeup of the executive management team, where it is probably sensible to include the head of each significant department or function. But it does not necessarily follow that the same arrangement must be adhered to at board level, even though it may have worked fairly well earlier on in the company's development. A radical consideration of such a board structure might suggest having the chief executive/MD, the finance director and perhaps just one or possibly two other key executive directors, and two or more well-chosen non-executives, plus the chairman. The balance of the board and the calibre and capability of the directors to contribute effectively to the board's work are of crucial importance here. These factors far outweigh the benefit of always having some operational knowledge readily available. If the board needs to have a first-hand opinion on any operational matter from time to time, in addition to that of the chief executive/MD, a senior executive can be asked to make a report to the board and answer questions on it, if necessary. It may be pertinent here to consider what the *Combined Code* has to say on board balance, which is summarized here:

- The board should include a balance of executive and non-executive directors (and in particular independent non-executive directors[1]) so that no individual or small group of individuals can dominate the board's decision making.
- The board should not be so large as to be unwieldy. The board should be of sufficient size that the balance of skills and experience is appropriate for the requirements of the business and that the changes to the board's composition can be managed without undue disruption. To ensure that power and information are not concentrated in one or two individuals, there should be a strong presence on the board of both executive and non-executive directors.

CHOOSING DIRECTORS

Although the whole board should agree to the appointment of a new director, the chairman or a nomination committee of the board would usually take the lead in the selection process. At the start of the process it is important to determine what roles the new person is to fulfil as a board member and what personal characteristics would be appropriate. An analysis of these factors for existing board members can help to identify gaps and can be particularly useful to help identify the strengths that you would want to see in a new

1 The board should determine whether the director is independent in character and judgement and whether there are relationships or circumstances which are likely to affect, or could appear to affect, the director's judgement. See page 205 in Appendix 2 for the full code definition of independence.

appointee to the board. The diagnostic chart in Figure 5.1 can be utilized to help identify the strengths and weaknesses of your board in terms of both the directors' personal characteristics and the roles that they can play, using the lists shown in the first section of this chapter.

Start by putting the initials of each board member, including yourself, at the head of one of the columns on the chart. Then, consider each of the personal characteristics described on page 90 in the first section of this chapter (against numbers 1–12 on the chart) in relation to the director identified in the first column and put a tick against those where he or she is strong. Repeat this process for each of the directors. Then consider the 12 roles that directors play, described later in the same section on page 96 (against letters A–L on the chart), and indicate those fulfilled strongly by each director

Directors:										
Characteristics										
1										
2										
3										
4										
5										
6										
7										
8										
9										
10										
11										
12										
Roles										
A										
B										
C										
D										
E										
F										
G										
H										
I										
J										
K										
L										

Figure 5.1 Board diagnostic chart

in the same way on the chart. Once completed, you will be able to see at a glance where the gaps are and also where your board is 'overweight'. Then decide which of the gaps need to be strengthened on your board by a new appointee and include these factors in the job specification, which will also, of course, take other factors into account.

Selecting executive directors

When selecting a person for appointment as an executive director, one needs to look for a number of important characteristics and personal qualities that are necessary to perform the role effectively. Even when a person has won his or her spurs by accepting a high level of responsibility as an executive or manager, it does not necessarily follow that he or she will be able to fulfil effectively the more demanding and different role of director.

All directors must be able to contribute to the board's affairs on a broad spectrum of matters, rather than seeing things from a specialist's viewpoint. They must be capable of looking beyond the confines of their own particular discipline or background and have the breadth of vision and thinking necessary to help the board address the policy and strategic issues, as well as all the operational matters.

It is important that a director can work as a member of a team – a board. This requires certain interpersonal skills, including the ability to listen and understand not only what others are saying but also the reasons why things are sometimes left unsaid. This borders on the topic of boardroom politics, so that someone who is politically naive, who is blunt and lacks sensitivity, may find the boardroom environment a difficult one to succeed in. Just as it is important to listen, so the director must have an ability to express ideas, concepts and facts in a succinct way, and have the patience and understanding to accommodate the varying knowledge horizons of co-directors.

Financial awareness and numeracy are required of all directors and, in the case of quoted companies, knowledge of how the stock market works. A knowledge of corporate affairs, including sources and methods of funding, must also be acquired. In these areas, the basic capability needs to be already possessed by the executive director, but specific knowledge can and should be acquired before or soon after appointment.

Whether an executive director is selected from within the same company or group, or recruited from outside, some education and training in the role of the director and how the board works may well be necessary. However, as with all training, selecting the right person first, with all the attributes for the job, is an essential prerequisite.

When evaluating potential candidates, weighting will be given to an established track record of achievement. It is also important to check how well the person is respected by his or her peers, subordinates and superiors. A successful candidate should have motivational and behavioural characteristics that are appropriate to the appointment. While these can be ascertained to some extent during interview and by personal references, subjective judgements in this area can often be wrong. Consequently, the use of one of the more comprehensive psychometric test procedures can add a useful dimension of objectivity to the selection process.

Selecting non-executive directors

It is the non-executive directors who provide the variable element in achieving a well-balanced and competent board. Each will therefore be chosen with regard to the balance of skills, experience and approach, since the board should constitute an integrated team to shape the destiny of the company, ensure its profitable performance and safeguard its interests. So the selection of each non-executive director should be made with care, taking account of the strengths and weaknesses of the other directors and the major issues likely to be addressed by the board in the years ahead.

Essentially, a non-executive director should provide an independent and impartial view of the board's considerations and decisions while also identifying strongly with the company's affairs. It is essential, therefore, to look for strength of character and an ability to stand back from the issue being considered, combined with an essential pragmatism and ability to compromise. This calls for personal qualities of courage, integrity, common sense, good judgement, tenacity, diplomacy, and an ability to listen carefully and to communicate with clarity, objectivity and brevity.

The particular background, experience and any special disciplines that would be appropriate to a particular appointment will naturally depend on the qualities of the other directors of the board and the particular business concerned. Experience of a larger, unrelated but relevant enterprise, with knowledge of company matters and board competence gained in another environment, is often needed. A sharp business mind with an ability to focus on the matters in hand without historical or day-to-day distractions is essential. Selecting someone with an established track record is usually wise, since opinions at the board table will benefit from the weight of that experience. Numeracy and an ability to gain an adequate understanding of the company's finances, management, employees, special capabilities and markets should be ascertained when selecting a non-executive director.

The board's total effectiveness can benefit from outside contacts and opinions. One will therefore often seek non-executive directors who have a suitable network of experienced contacts.

Many chairmen use their non-executive directors to provide personal counsel and a different perspective on matters of concern, before they are raised at board meetings. You will probably also want to use the non-executive directors to advise on the remuneration of executive directors, and perhaps your own, often dealt with in committees. Where this is the case, the appropriate experience, knowledge and personal qualities should be looked for.

The report by Derek Higgs on the 'Role and Effectiveness of Non-Executive Directors' (2003) identified issues and practices that can help to raise boardroom effectiveness. This work has been augmented by the 'Tyson Report' on the recruitment and development of non-executive directors (June 2003). Both documents can be useful references (See Appendix 2). This later report highlights how a range of different backgrounds, skills and experiences among board members can enhance board effectiveness and explores how a broader range of non-executive directors can be identified and recruited. It demonstrates how board diversity can also send a positive and motivating signal to customers, shareholders and employees, and can contribute to a better understanding by the company's leadership of the diverse constituencies that affect its success.

It advocates that many UK companies would benefit from extending their searches for NEDs to new pools of talent and that broader, more rigorous and more transparent search processes would enhance board effectiveness while also fostering greater diversity in the background, experience, age, gender, ethnicity and nationality of NEDs. Training and evaluation processes are likely to be particularly important for companies committed to building diverse boards and to realizing the benefits of diversity among their members, and the report explores this.

The valuable contribution of non-executive directors can usually raise the level of discussion and decision making of the board. Their selection should therefore be carried out with the same care and professionalism used in selecting executive directors and senior executives, and this is usually best done with professional outside help.

The following extract on interviewing non-executive director candidates is from an article by Patrick Dunne (1999) that appeared in *The Independent Director.*

Interviewing candidates

So how do you tell whether someone has good judgement from an interview? Track record clearly provides an indication, but the first signal you get when you meet them is that they will find it hard to get in the door because of the size of their ears; they are great listeners and are unlikely to drone on about the people they know or famous past victories.

They will behave like good independent directors in the interview, listening carefully and asking short but thought-provoking questions. They will try to get a good feel for your strategy for the business and the ownership. By talking through current issues you should also get a feel for their influencing style and whether they can be trusted.

Bear in mind that it is hard to influence people who don't respect you – no matter how user-friendly you are. An impressive track record may help generate respect, but real respect comes through the combination of achievement and personality.

What sort of personality should you be looking for? Good listening skills have been mentioned earlier. Two other vital attributes are vigour and rigour. Gaining proper familiarity with a business and becoming a valued member of the board team requires considerable commitment. In order to be of real use in discussing complex issues, a rigorous mind and one that is good at absorbing information is also required.

A 'cuddle and kick' personality is needed. You must find someone who will provide both encouragement as well as ensuring that there is appropriate corporate governance. Confident humility and calm wisdom are traits of the natural confidant. You should feel able to confide in your independent director and he or she should have the confidence to debate the things closest to your business heart. It may also be worth considering why he or she is prepared to join your board and what the motivation is. The best reasons are seldom financial. This is not to say they won't want to be fairly rewarded, just that interest in your business and a passion for the business world are vitally important.

One final characteristic of a good independent director is recognizing when it is time to go. Perhaps this is the ultimate proof of good judgement.

A characteristic of those who succeed in picking really effective independent directors is that they research their candidates with skill and care. They make sure they talk to other directors who have them on their boards.

'You could really do with a decent non-executive director.' This often well-intended remark is received in a variety of ways. Many hear it as implied criticism, others – usually those doing well – fail to see its relevance. The wise listen and, if it is right, turn it into an opportunity.

Selecting directors – summary of qualities to look for

- Capability to take a wider view than confined by their background or discipline.
- Political astuteness and sensitivity.
- Good interpersonal skills.
- Ability to listen and to communicate ideas, concepts and facts succinctly and emphatically.
- Financial awareness and numeracy.
- Business competence.
- Good judgement, common sense, diplomacy.
- Strength of character, courage, integrity, wisdom.*
- Relevant experience, special knowledge and skills.*

*These qualities are particularly important in non-executive directors, who should also display independence, objectivity and an ability to stay focused on the matters in hand.

Experienced chairmen expressed the following views on some of the topics covered in this section

Sir Nigel Mobbs

Some chairmen find getting hold of the right non-executive directors is difficult. We tend to use the personal networks of our non-executive directors and myself to identify suitable candidates, once we have agreed a specification of what we want in terms of skills, experience and personality. This may sound a bit incestuous, but it actually works quite effectively. The fact is you don't want someone you know too well. But head-hunters can be useful if you and your colleagues don't know of suitable people.

Linda Smith

There is an issue in the health service at the moment concerning how far the chair can actually choose the non-executive directors. I have always found it possible to choose my own, although they have to be submitted by the regional chair to the minister. I've got the people I want, mainly because I have been able to put people forward, any of whom I would be happy with. But there is a problem around the current system of taking from a regional database and a regional pool, where they are interviewed regionally and then we are asked to meet them but not to interview them. So you are just looking at fit, not whether or not they would make a good non-executive director – that has been done already. But I don't think it always works and I have met some weak candidates through this process who would not, I think, be suitable at all.

Either we are appointed and paid as chairs to be accountable and to manage our boards, or we are not. An important part of our role is to choose the people who would be a good team and to get the balance right, and we are not entirely free to do that. So I think this is a problem to be resolved.

PLANNING AND MANAGING CHANGES

As chairman, in helping to shape the vision of tomorrow's company, you must consider how the board should be expanded or reduced in size and developed, strengthened and balanced to tackle the scale, complexity and scope of issues that lie ahead. This requires a board development plan to address the changing needs of the board and the company's evolution, with key events and timescales. You may find the questions posed in the following checklist useful when carrying out this task.

Board development plan checklist

- Does the board really add sufficient value to the company? Is it a professional board, able to reach consensus after tough-minded, penetrating exploration of issues, obtained by non-adversarial discussion? What might be done to improve matters?
- Does the board work well together in its present configuration?
- Will the existing board be competent to direct the company in the future, given the likely objectives, challenges and opportunities?
- Is the current size of the board appropriate, given the scope and complexity of issues likely to face the company and the need for good board dynamics?
- Is the balance between executive and non-executive directors the most appropriate? Should there be more or fewer non-executive members, recognizing both the importance of their contributions and the need for a well-balanced, dynamic team?
- Are a sufficient number of the non-executive directors genuinely independent of the company? Do they all still make an effective contribution?
- Are any directors really not good enough for the job and are changes needed?
- What views do the other directors have about the present board structure and capability? Is there likely to be support or opposition to changes?
- Is there a separate chairman and chief executive/MD? If not, is the current situation the more desirable, given the future challenges?
- Is there a succession plan for the board?

Experienced chairmen expressed the following views on some of the topics covered in this section

Michael Mander

If the argument for limiting the length of service on a board was that you should be bringing in new ideas, I can buy that. But the removal of a non-executive director after say 10 years as a matter of principle is, I think, wrong. After all, that 10 years' experience of the company can be a huge advantage. So I think that a limit to the length of service or an age limit should not be applied. Where two non-executive directors have been on the board for a long time and are still adding value and making useful contributions relevant to the company's future, why change them for the sake of it? A better course of action would be to recruit a third one to bring in new ideas and a different experience profile.

One role of the chairman in a smaller board can be leading the nomination committee. There must be a proper succession plan, where such questions as, 'What happens if the chief executive/MD gets run over by a bus?' are addressed. I don't agree that a senior non-executive director should be appointed as a 'whistle blower'. I think this is divisive and can cause bad blood to exist where it didn't exist before – and it is totally unnecessary. I can go along with the idea of the appointment of a deputy chairman, particularly when the roles of chairman and chief executive/MD are combined. On the other hand, where the chairman is a separate appointment I think the appointment of a deputy should not be mandatory.

Sir Nigel Mobbs

As to planning changes of non-executive directors, I don't believe that they necessarily lose independence and effectiveness over time. A lot depends on the energy they can bring to the job and the commitment they still have to taking on a challenge and at times precipitating one. It's a matter of whether they are still making a good contribution to the board's work.

CHAPTER CHECKLIST

Here are some questions you might ask yourself in connection with the matters covered in this chapter before you plan any consequent action:

- What changes need to be made to your current board if it is to fully meet the variety and complexity of challenges that lie ahead?

- ... does it possess the depth of experience and personal characteristics to address the future 'conditioning' tasks comprehensively?
- ... and will it be able to address the scale and complexity of the 'enterprise' tasks to ensure that proper advantage is taken of likely opportunities?
- Where a director is nominated to sit on your board, do you insist on more than one candidate, so that the most appropriate one can be selected?
- Will you undertake a full appraisal to determine the personal characteristics that are deficient in your present board and seek to fill the gaps when new recruits are sought?
- Will you examine what knowledge and experience will be needed and identify where the shortages are?
- Will you try to attain a high degree of board balance with regard to personal characteristics, special knowledge and experience, directors' roles and executive/non-executive directors?
- Will directors who don't add real value to the board be developed or replaced with more able people?
- Are you aiming to achieve a well-balanced board of high calibre and competence?
- Is your board of appropriate size and, if not, will you take action to achieve well-informed insights and decision making?
- Is the structure of your board appropriate for the future and, if not, will you initiate the required changes?
- When choosing new directors, will you bear in mind the qualities listed on page 110?
- Do you intend to draw up a board development plan to bring about any necessary changes to your board's composition in a timely way?

6

Managing the board's business

PLANNING BOARD MEETINGS

At the centre of your management of the board's business is the conduct of the meetings where the directors come together formally to address their work. These are the occasions when your skills as the board's leader will be tested and when all the planning and preparation you have carried out pays off. It is surprising, therefore, that many chairmen pay insufficient attention to ensuring that the scene will be set to give the best opportunity for all board meetings to be fully effective. Thoughtful planning is the basis for effective, successful meetings.

How long and when?

Perhaps the first questions to address relate to the duration, frequency and timing of board meetings.

Most well-conducted, effective 'proper' board meetings have a duration of two to four hours. (By 'proper', I mean focused exclusively on board matters, where significant authority is delegated to management, without requiring routine detailed and comprehensive reporting and discussion of operational performance at board meetings.) After all, the interest, attention and energy levels of most people at any meeting decline significantly after a few hours and directors are no exception. Indeed, fresh minds are needed to address the most important issues facing the organization – issues that will determine its future prosperity and ensure that its interests and reputation are safeguarded. If your board meetings tend to go on for too long, it is probably for one or more of the following reasons, all of which you can do something about:

- they are not 'proper' board meetings (see the definition of 'proper' above);
- the agendas are too full, perhaps because meetings are not frequent enough;
- procedures at meetings are protracted and cumbersome;
- board behaviour allows unfocused and irrelevant discussion;
- chairmanship of meetings is poor.

The frequency of your board meetings will to some extent be governed by the amount of business to be conducted. If you currently hold meetings quarterly or bimonthly and agendas are usually too crowded, consider increasing the frequency. On the other hand, board meetings do not have to be held each month just because a set of accounts is available monthly or because executive management meetings are convened that often. Bimonthly meetings are often the most appropriate. In many cases the use of committees of the board to consider certain matters in depth outside board meetings can be a useful way of limiting the time required to cover the necessary business. We will touch on the use of committees of the board towards the end of this chapter.

Some forethought should be given to the timing of board meetings in relation to the annual cycle. The start and finish of the annual accounting period is usually used as a reference point for when the board should sign off the year's accounts and also when strategic plans and budgets for the new year should be approved. Many boards use these events to mark the timing of related board meetings and structure other matters into the agendas of intervening meetings to give a fairly even balance of content for the agendas of the next year's meetings.

Agendas

The agenda for a board meeting is a valuable tool to help you keep everyone's mind focused on the achievement of the required outcomes. It should set out the structure of the meeting in a clear and unambiguous way for all the directors to see and refer to, giving impartial support to your authority during the meeting. Make sure it is always sent out well ahead of the meeting.

Although, as chairman, you should take responsibility for what will be on the agenda for each meeting, remember that it is the *board's* agenda and be open to suggestions for inclusion of items from any director and the company secretary. Perhaps your main task here is to ensure that all issues that the board needs to consider are included at an appropriate time and that these are all proper matters for the board. Try not to put too many topics on any one agenda that are each likely to require a substantial amount of time to consider and discuss. This will avoid the likelihood of those meetings becoming protracted or rushed.

The list of a board's reserved powers shown as an example in Chapter 3 provides the following checklist of topics that might appear on a board's agenda. Some will be in the form of proposals or requests for the board's consideration and/or agreement, some will be topics for review and some might appear under either heading, depending on the circumstances. Some will occur on all or most agendas, some annually and others at the appropriate time.

Checklist of topics for board agendas

- the company's objectives, vision, mission and goals;
- strategies and strategic plans;
- annual budgets;
- regular reviews of performance against budgets and plans;
- any matter that would have a material effect on the company's financial position, liabilities, future strategy or reputation;
- major capital projects in excess of (x value);
- capital expenditure in excess of budgets;
- changes to the company's capital structure;

- significant changes in accounting, risk management, capital and treasury policies and practices, including foreign exchange exposures;
- significant changes to the company's financial and management control systems;
- capital expenditure, disposals, acquisitions and joint ventures above the authority levels delegated to the chief executive/MD;
- the establishment and annual review of such delegated authority levels;
- contracts not in the ordinary course of business and material contracts in the ordinary course of business;
- net borrowings in excess of peak budgeted or forecasted levels;
- dividends to shareholders;
- financial statements, including interim and Annual Reports and Accounts;
- circulars and prospectuses to shareholders, including listing arrangements and those convening general meetings, except circulars of a routine nature;
- review of auditor's letter of recommendations;
- changes to the Memorandum and Articles of Association;
- reappointment or change of auditors;
- approval of audit fee;
- approval of auditor's engagement letter and scope of audit;
- the issue of ordinary and preference shares;
- share option schemes;
- appointment and removal of directors and company secretary, including those of subsidiaries;
- powers, roles and duties delegated to individual directors, including the chairman, chief executive/MD and finance director;
- remuneration and terms of appointment of directors and senior executives, including bonus arrangements, share options, pensions and contracts of employment;
- terms of reference and membership of board committees;

- material changes in pension scheme rules;
- liability insurance arrangements for directors and officers of the company;
- compliance with contracts, laws, statutory obligations and regulations;
- company policies on probity, ethics;
- the company Code of Conduct;
- company policies on employment matters, matters concerning the physical environment, communication and reputation management, risk management and internal control.

During a board meeting you must concentrate almost entirely on its process, rather than its substance. Consequently, you should take time to focus more on its substance before the meeting. Forming preliminary opinions on all major issues well before each meeting can help you do this, even though you may change your mind afterwards. In order to structure the meeting effectively you must try to assess the amount of discussion each agenda item will require. You may decide that some matters need further refinement or information before coming to the board, some may be contentious and others could call on the full problem solving capability of the board. This prejudgement, however tentative, will help you to plan the agenda, guide the board's deliberations, keep control of the meeting and ensure that it does not overrun.

Some chairmen ask the company secretary to draft out each agenda as a starting point, based on a previously agreed template, which will include any major items on the annual schedule. It is good practice to discuss and agree the agenda with the chief executive/MD and the company secretary before it is finalized. Both will probably have practical insights and suggestions to augment your own and a consensus between the three of you will give added integrity to the final list.

When considering the order in which to include items on the agenda for a meeting, it is sensible to put those topics that will require a decision from the board near the beginning. This arrangement allows the directors to deal with these matters when their minds are freshest and affords the opportunity for you to give as much time as is needed to these, the most important matters on the agenda. If, as a consequence of an over-long discussion near the start, time is short for items appearing later on the agenda, it will be of less concern. In that event, some of the less important later matters may easily be held over until the next meeting. It is also good practice to indicate on the agenda which items are for decision and which for discussion or consideration only.

Many chairmen follow the practice of not including an 'any other business' item on the agenda. This encourages board members to think about agenda items and to suggest them for inclusion ahead of meetings. It also allows the chairman to keep control of the meetings and avoid messy, even rushed, conclusions to them.

Physical factors

To get the best outcomes from your board meetings you must pay attention to various physical factors that can have an impact on their performance.

Have you ever considered how the shape of the board table and where individuals sit around it can affect the dynamics of the meetings? When seven or more people sit around a long, thin table, there can easily be a sense of separation rather than cohesion. This climate is exacerbated when the group is particularly large. If a 'power group' exists at one end of the table, those near the other end may feel somewhat isolated or even excluded. These are quite subtle matters but they can have an unconscious impact on the climate in which board meetings take place.

If there is no option but to use a long, thin table, then sit in the middle of one of the long sides rather than at the end. Better still, insist on using a round, oval or square table. In any case, avoid the impression of a power group by having the chief executive / MD and the finance director sit apart from one another and away from you, rather than both at your side. You can help to create a sense of cohesion, rather than division, by determining who sits where in relation to whom. Mix up the executive and non-executive directors, rather than let them sit in groups, particularly on opposite sides of the table. Use place names at the board table so that *you* can determine who sits where.

Directors should be able to concentrate all their mental energy on the matters to be considered at board meetings. They may find this focus difficult to maintain if the physical environment is poor. You should consider all of the following factors and ensure that they are met:

- The air in the room must be at a comfortable temperature and refreshed throughout the meeting to ensure that a good oxygen level is maintained.
- There should be freedom from extraneous noise and interruptions – insist that only true emergency messages be brought in.
- Make sure that the room is well lit and is equipped with comfortable chairs that have good lumbar support and well-cushioned seats.
- The board table should be large enough to give everyone adequate room to spread out their papers and turn in their chair, without encroaching on the area occupied by their next door neighbour.
- Plenty of fresh water and drinking glasses should be provided on the board table, perhaps with a side table carrying fresh coffee and cups too.
- During the meetings, create 'comfort breaks' that give everyone opportunities to 'stretch their legs', get a cup of coffee and visit the lavatory, so helping to maintain levels of concentration and energy.

Help from the company secretary

A close relationship between the company secretary and the chairman of the board can be critical to the effective running and management of a board. In principle, both can play their part in the smooth running of board meetings. Essentially, the chairman is responsible for the overall management and conduct of the board, whereas the company secretary is involved in the mechanics of its organization and processes.

The *Combined Code* on corporate governance stressed the importance of the role of the company secretary in the following way:

> *Under the direction of the chairman, the company secretary's responsibilities include ensuring good information flows within the board and its committees*

and between senior management and non-executive directors, as well as facilitating induction and assisting with professional development as required.

The company secretary should be responsible for advising the board through the chairman on all governance matters.

Duties of a company secretary usually include:

- the convening of the board and company meetings;
- advising the chairman on the agenda for board meetings;
- taking minutes of meetings;
- writing up the company's statutory books: register of members, register of directors, register of directors' interests, directors' service contracts, minute book of general meetings, minute book of board meetings;
- filing returns with the Registrar of Companies;
- communicating with shareholders;
- dealing with share transfers and monitoring share movements;
- guidance on ensuring compliance with relevant regulations;
- administering any alterations to the Memorandum or Articles of Association.

Information for the board

The effectiveness of board meetings will be greatly affected by the written information provided to directors in preparation for them. I cannot over-emphasize the importance of good preparation for meetings and would urge you to *always* insist that *all* the information that relates to a meeting is available to the directors at least five days in advance. (Of course, there may well be occasions when very recent updates would be apposite too.) This gives every director time to read and understand the information, seek clarification where necessary and form a preliminary view about each topic. This pre-meeting process is an essential part of good group decision making and forms the basis of thorough, penetrating discussion. Your board cannot expect to work effectively if this preparation process is impaired or does not take place at all.

The form and substance of board information will also influence the effectiveness of the board meetings. That is why you should have the board agree some 'rules of presentation' concerning how matters must be presented when being given to board members as papers for meetings. The board should also agree the timeliness of having them available to the company secretary, or whoever else sends out the board papers. In this way, there can be no excuse for reports and proposals that are late or in the wrong form. Once agreed, put it all in writing and give each director a copy.

Such rules of presentation might stipulate that proposals for the board to consider and / or decide upon should be contained concisely on a few pages at most. This should include a front-page summary with, where appropriate, unambiguous recommendations. The proposal should argue the case, with concepts clearly stated and their source and that of supporting data identified. Any assumptions that have been made and the reasons for doing so should also be stated. If the matter has been considered in depth and recommended by a committee of the board or a project team, this fact should be stated, together with an indication of the extent and soundness of their investigations or considerations.

Where the matter to be presented is quite complex or represents a problem for the board to consider and help to resolve, visual presentation material, supported by a verbal explanation, is often appropriate. The rule here should be that audiovisual presentations are limited to a maximum time of, say, 5 or 10 minutes and kept to essentials. Focus should also be kept on the matter being presented, rather than trying to dazzle with the full range of features that are available from computer-based presentation aids. Supporting written material should be included in the papers for the meeting.

Whatever rules are made about proposals and reports being presented to the board, there will be times when a purely verbal report may be the most appropriate. Such occasions may occur when security is necessary or when an idea or concept is being put forward that is ill-formed and would benefit from the insights of other board members at the formative stage. In such cases, it should be for the chairman to decide when the rules might be bent. You can insist that the matter be presented in a concise, well-articulated manner and prescribe a time limit for the topic to be discussed, particularly if the idea is new. A firmer proposal can then be made for discussion at a subsequent meeting.

You must also consider the 'rules of presentation' for matters that are to be reviewed by the board and for the routine reporting of company performance. Here one is looking for reports that are sufficiently comprehensive to be informative, yet presented concisely so that the directors can focus on the important matters that may need their collective consideration.

The reports on compliance with company policies and similar matters should cover all the relevant areas in the company, highlighting any topics of actual or potential concern and any consequent action that is being taken. The methods used to conduct the assessment and the scope of their application should be stated, together with which people were responsible. This is an area where the board may sometimes ask for independent audits to be carried out, when prior guidance on the preferred form of report for the board might be given.

In setting up committees that report to the board, the board should decide the form, substance and frequency of reporting. The chairman of the committee will usually prepare these reports. Where a committee undertakes tasks on behalf of the board it should identify where it considers action or improvement is needed and to recommend the steps to be taken.

Much of the reporting on performance should relate to the performance indicators that the board has already agreed (see Chapter 3). Having decided what degree of variance is permissible in each case, the reports should focus on whether these limits have been or are likely to be exceeded. Where appropriate, the written text that supports the figures should explain any excess variance from expected results or trends and what action is being undertaken to correct it. The reports on the 'softer' topics relating to the achievement of strategic objectives and related changes will usually come in the form of periodic short written reports. These would usually cover what is happening, what has been achieved and a forecast, with a summary of any supporting information. The board may also call for occasional audits in these areas, particularly if some degree of uncertainty exists.

It is usual to have a report from the chief executive/MD at each board meeting. In most cases this is included as a written report in the papers for the meeting, but some boards rely on verbal reports. In either case, the report should refer to the underlying health of the business, the degree to which expectations are being realized, significant problems, threats and opportunities in prospect and any major changes in the environment in which the company operates. It should be limited to matters of interest or concern to the board and be brief. It will become clear to you at the meeting which matters will require consequent discussion and you will doubtless have formed your own views as to which they will be.

The finance director will usually provide a report for each board meeting in written form, for inclusion in the board papers. This should be brief and to the point, illustrating the financial position of the organization. It should state cash flow, borrowings and other major financial parameters, which may be brought up to date verbally at the meeting if appropriate. Forecasts and trends could usually be included, where the use of charts, graphs and ratios can often give extra clarity. Ask your finance director to keep the presentation of the data simple, without blinding everyone with figures, and to interpret the important issues in the short written text that should accompany the figures.

Experienced chairmen expressed the following views on some of the topics covered in this section

Michael Mander

I don't think any board meeting should go on for more than three to three-and-a-half hours. The laws of diminishing returns take place and I see that, unquestionably, the most effective meetings are those that don't last too long. That is where the chairman's role is very important in trying to make sure that the discussion of critical issues is not cut short, but on the other hand that the total board meeting runs to time. I have been on boards where the meetings went on for twice as long as they needed to because the chairman allowed people to ramble. It is important that the chairman makes sure the agenda for a meeting is appropriate and limited to proper board issues. On one of my boards the secretary is very good and gives me a draft agenda, where he will include what he knows of what is going on. Sometimes an executive or non-executive director will suggest things to go on the agenda and, although I am the final arbiter of what is included, I can't recall ever having had to say no. The chief executive sees the draft agenda too and I also have a conversation with him to tell me of any contentious matters that are going on in the company. He often says he would rather not, for fear it might prejudice open discussion.

Sir Nigel Mobbs

Getting the agenda right, and the papers that go with it, is vital for an effective board meeting. We have a board meeting schedule for the year so that we know broadly what items of a routine nature will be on the agenda each month. Other items can then be added, but it does set out the plan framework for the year. This meetings schedule is copied to each director so that they know when certain reports are due. At each meeting there is a routine report by the individual executive directors about their area of responsibility, including the finance director, plus a chief executive's report. There is also a slot for me to report on anything I feel is relevant for each meeting, although often there is nothing to say.

If there is a major paper to come before the board it should be prefaced by a 'warning paper' that sets the scene for what will be issued for the meeting. Too many chairmen are not disciplined enough about the pre-delivery of board papers. We send out our papers 10 days ahead of the meeting, but in any case there should be a weekend to read them. The papers should be clear enough so that a decision can almost be made based on what is in the paper, with the salient details contained in two or three pages at most.

I think that the chairman must be involved in the approval of the agenda that finally goes out and the papers that go with it. The company secretary prepares it on my instructions and will show it to the chief executive before publication. If the chief executive wanted something included, he would have asked me. Suggestions for items to be included are usually made informally, often at board meetings – 'Wouldn't it be a good idea to…'. I always meet the non-executive directors for half an hour over coffee before board meetings and sometimes suggestions are made there too. Because these pre-board meetings are a regular feature, the executive directors do not see them as a private cabal that might divide the board into two camps. They help to clarify things and inform – we certainly don't decide anything there.

Dennis Woods

We fix dates for board meetings a year ahead that are sacrosanct. We use a pretty standard agenda, so most things are covered under the general headings. But if there are specific issues for discussion, they are put onto the agenda too and any director can suggest items for the agenda – and they frequently do. We avoid spending too much time at board meetings looking at the past by distributing the figures and the accounts ahead of the meeting and only discussing exceptional results. Generally, our board tends to look forward all the time – which is where our focus is.

Linda Smith

If, as chair, you don't manage the business and the agenda of the board, then what often happens is that decisions that have to be made get made outside the board.

I find the planning of board meetings difficult because of the weight of business that we have. So we are looking at ways of reducing the range of things that we normally do by delegating some of them for directors to handle. This will help us to try to concentrate on our strategic issues – shaping, pushing forward and modernizing the health service, our accountability and things we have to deliver, and not get bogged down in all the other things.

Our board meetings are in two parts. The private part lasts about one hour and the public part about three hours. That's really too long and people start to get tired. It is important to get the agenda right, so that issues are addressed at the appropriate time, and we use an annual framework to facilitate this. There are some specific matters that must be dealt with at certain times and in between we handle the shaping of specific things that are being developed. The trick is to retain, in that process, our strategic role and focusing on the things that we think are important in that and not just discussing it all. Achieving that is exceedingly difficult, because there are so many topics. I don't think you ever get this right, but struggle with it.

I have a meeting each week with the chief executive and the board secretary where we update on what's happening. We look at what things we might need to put on the board agenda and consider when we might need to have away-days or have a special meeting to bite off a particular difficult issue.

CONDUCTING BOARD MEETINGS

The chairman as leader and guide

Your primary concerns should be the cohesion of the board, the integrity of the meeting process, the achievement of the board's purpose and objectives and the goals of the company as a whole. These are best achieved by displaying respect, patience, humour and goodwill. The less you are seen to impose your views on others, the more able you will be to lead the board effectively. Perhaps your most important attribute is an ability to listen well – being aware of what is said and the reasoning behind it. The less you say about particular matters at board meetings, the greater your strength. Lead and guide – concentrate on the quality and aptness of your comments to achieve this.

During meetings you should try to remain neutral, otherwise you will inhibit the input from others. If you argue your own position you will have difficulty paying attention to guiding the process. Never divert your attention and concentration by attempting to take the minutes of a meeting – always leave that job to a competent secretary.

Most of the really effective and successful chairmen you might have met will have developed the skills to motivate and lead in a positive way. They will be adept at listening, to hear what their fellow directors are truly saying and to sense when there is discord and confusion or harmony and agreement. They will also be able to bring people and ideas together in a constructive way. The capacity to approach people, relationships and problems in terms of the present rather than the past and to accept people as they are, not as they might be, are characteristics of such chairmen. They are trusting of their colleagues and succeed without the need or wish for frequent approval and recognition for what they do. You may wish to emulate such people.

Your effectiveness in the role of the board's leader will be influenced by the courtesy you display towards your fellow directors. Not only will your courtesy be seen as a sign of respect, setting an example of good behaviour for others, but it also allows you more freedom to be direct and tough when the situation demands, without appearing discourteous.

Being courteous allows you some room to make mistakes without losing the respect of the other board members and puts your comments in the most favourable light. It is also a means of persuasion in itself, for many are persuaded by manner as much as reason. You will doubtless recognize the following common courtesies in dealing with your fellow directors, particularly at board meetings:

- Show concern for the welfare and personal life of your fellow directors.
- Make sure the meeting environment is comfortable and conducive to good work.
- Go out of your way for newcomers and the more reticent.
- Listen attentively.
- Give credit when it is due.
- Don't praise yourself.
- Learn to give and accept a compliment.
- Don't embarrass others in public.
- As its leader, accept blame for the whole board.

Any influence you want to have on the outcome of any matter on the agenda of a board meeting should be achieved with subtlety and care. Depending on your goal, your first method should be to see to what extent you can narrow the issue or get it decided in your favour prior to the meeting, so as to avoid using your authority when chairing it. If you want a particular point to be advocated strongly at the meeting, you should enlist another member to make that point whenever you can. You will be more effective supporting someone else's point than making your own. Only when all other efforts fail should you attempt to influence the outcome by expressing substantive opinions. In the end, your continuing effectiveness as chairman is more important than your dominating the board on any one issue. You should not sacrifice the former for the latter.

Generally, where there is little or no disagreement on an opinion that you agree with anyway, you should avoid involving yourself in the discussion. Similarly, it is probably unwise to try to persuade the board to your point of view at a meeting where there is obvious overwhelming opposition to it. Such influence is best attempted before the meeting takes place. Only on highly important issues or those affecting fundamental matters should you marshal all your energies to influence decisions.

How can you maintain discipline in a board meeting to keep the meeting on track? Whatever your source of power, your real and worthwhile authority will come from your perceived commitment to the board as a group and to its objectives, as well as from your skill in guiding the group to meet those objectives. This authority will be limited if you are perceived to have your own agenda, or to favour some directors over others. On the other hand, your authority will be stronger if you show a real commitment to every member of the board and the board's objectives. This even-handed approach will give you the tacit authority of the whole board to deal with an individual director who may be endangering the process. You will be seen as imposing not your own will, but rather that of the board as a group. As such, your voice will represent those of others and your authority will be all the greater.

Try to imagine the agenda issues and the required outcomes in your head shortly before the meeting takes place. This foresight, together with an intrinsic understanding of the strategic goals, the objectives to be achieved and the steps to be taken to achieve them, will help you greatly to give the necessary leadership and guidance during the meeting. If you can convey the essence of these matters to the board members as you proceed, you will help them to keep the meeting focused to achieve the desired outcomes.

Chairing board meetings

Always arrive before the meeting is due to start. This allows you to interact informally with everyone before the more formal proceedings begin and ensures that you are ordered and composed, updating yourself on any matters that might affect the meeting prior to the start. Then make sure the meeting begins on time. By doing so you establish your control and your professional, businesslike approach to the affairs of the day and set the ground rules for others to follow. Only in very exceptional circumstances should the start be delayed for latecomers. If your colleagues know that you always begin the board meetings on time and in a businesslike way, they are all the more likely to make a point of being early. If you know in advance that someone will arrive late, announce the fact at the beginning and don't allow the proceedings to be interrupted when he or she does arrive.

Start the meeting in a decisive, positive manner. Ask everyone to take their places at the board table and set an example by sitting down promptly yourself. Look around the table and meet everyone's eyes briefly and purposefully, then state formally that the meeting has begun, using a slightly raised voice if appropriate. Show strength and confidence in establishing that the business of the board has started and that you are in charge of the proceedings. Remind everyone of the items on the agenda, pointing out the important issues that will probably engage most of the board's attention and deliberations. By clarifying what needs to be achieved and when, at this stage of the meeting, you will help to focus the mind of the board as a group on the work to be done. It will also make everyone aware of the pacing needed to achieve the required outcomes from the meeting.

As the meeting progresses, briefly introduce each topic to set the scene for what transpires subsequently. Then pass the responsibility for opening a discussion or making a presentation to the person concerned, or table the matter for open discussion. Try to limit your comments to a sentence or two if you can. Your main function is to guide the board to making the best decisions it can by bringing out the best contributions to discussions from every director. This requires you to appear impartial, encouraging a range of views to be expressed without being influenced by your own overt opinions. Many chairmen have difficulty keeping quiet about their own views or holding them to the end of the discussions, but it is worth persevering to overcome this trait to get the best from the board.

Keep the discussion as open as possible. Actively look for latent disagreement, dissent, or signs of frustration or anger and deal with it there and then. Although you should not force people to speak, do encourage the more reticent board members to express opinions and lend their knowledge and experience to discussions. It is important that minority views are expressed whenever they might add value to the decision making process and you must positively afford opportunities for them to be heard.

Discussions sometimes get bogged down or lead towards wrong conclusions because beliefs and opinions are argued as though they were facts. You must watch out for these occurrences and question the truth or relevance of the views expressed, in a way that does not bring you into contention with other directors. Your skill will also be tested if you see the board stampeding towards a conclusion by taking the most recent statement as the final word to be said on the subject. On these occasions you can often encourage a broadening of discussion by reminding the board of a different opinion expressed earlier and not fully considered. Another method is to ask individuals to predict what problems might arise if the view expressed were adopted.

Keep control of the discussions. Ask questions to clarify matters that are unclear to avoid misinterpretation, saving time and arguments. Some board members may tend to be verbose, others may be strident or have hobby-horses they like to ride. In such cases you must intervene to keep matters relevant and focused. As a more democratic approach, some boards have agreed a 'red card rule', where any director can raise a red card if he or she feels that someone has spoken for too long or lost the point. A red card from another colleague provides the chairman with support to ask the speaker to conclude.

One of your most important functions as chairman is to facilitate communication at board meetings. This requires that you be constantly on the lookout for possible miscommunications, which you must do what you can to correct and prevent. Watch out for the following common tendencies that can cause communication problems at board meetings:

- People misunderstanding the context in which a statement is made.
- The use of words or expressions with unclear or ambiguous meanings.
- Board members generalizing to such an extent that any relevance in a particular case becomes lost.
- Individuals presuming that others understand what they are thinking and saying.
- People not really concentrating on what is being said. If most members are looking languid, call a break in the meeting to re-energize everyone.

You have a responsibility for helping the board to make the best use of the time available. While this requires that you keep the meeting moving forward at a steady pace, it is important that each agenda item is allowed as much time as it deserves. Keep one eye on the time and whenever you feel that an issue is ripe to conclude, draw matters together and offer a summary.

Technically, a board is ultimately governed by simple majority voting procedures, with the chairman often having a casting vote. However, boards are essentially mechanisms for generating a consensus and the need for a well-run board to vote is rare. Indeed, if a board is split on deciding an important issue, it is better to defer the decision for more consultation and/or information, rather than put it to a vote. This process and the subsequent further discussion will usually clarify what outcome is the most appropriate, which may be different from those which caused the original split. The board's decisions will have real credibility and support only if the whole board can feel committed to them.

As each item on the agenda has been concluded, clearly state what that conclusion is and make sure that everyone agrees that it is the board's consensus. This applies whatever form the conclusion takes. Then promptly introduce the next item, to give a sense of momentum and successful progress to the meeting. At the same time, be concerned for the comfort of the board members and the levels of energy they display and consider taking a break.

Try to finish on time. If necessary, defer some matters to a later meeting or get the board to delegate them to a small group of the directors to resolve after the meeting, where appropriate. The practice of starting and finishing on time will encourage all board members to be disciplined in how they use their time and that of their colleagues at the meeting. It will also endorse your authority as the board's leader and your colleagues' respect and support for you in that role.

An experienced chairman expressed the following views on some of the topics covered in this section

Dennis Woods

I try to run a fairly formal board meeting where it is clear that I am in charge of affairs because I show leadership. I want everyone involved in board discussions and decisions – it's no use having a lot of 'yes men' who leave all the decisions to me. Our board meetings can be quite vocally heated at times and I don't try for too much control, but I do bring the subjects in and make sure everyone has their say. If somebody sat quietly, or if I know someone has a view but perhaps hasn't expressed it, then I would try to get them involved. We certainly encourage input from everyone. Minutes should include enough text to show that people's points of view have come across. This encourages directors to speak up next time and it also helps to remind us why we made a particular decision and how we came to it. If there are backup papers there too, they can throw light on the circumstances prevailing at the time, that influenced our decision.

BOARDROOM BEHAVIOUR

However able and competent individual directors may be, it is how they coalesce as a group that will determine the realization of their full potential as a board and the quality of their collective decisions. The performance of a board will be conditioned by the culture, style or personality that it adopts. This is determined to a great extent by the personalities and attitudes of the individual directors – their interpersonal skills, 'chemistry', professionalism and personal motivations. Although the composition of the board is an important factor here, another is the conduct of the board members themselves. Your conduct as chairman and the behaviour of the other directors, both individually and collectively, will therefore have a crucial bearing on the success of the board.

Many boards adopt a set of 'rules of engagement', which everyone agrees to try to adhere to during board meetings. These rules help people to behave in ways that are conducive to exploring issues in a comprehensive and effective way, channelling emotional and intellectual energies positively, without losing a desirable degree of dynamic tension. They also help to keep meetings shorter and focused. Such a set of rules might include the following items:

Rules of engagement

- Everyone must arrive before the scheduled time to start.
- Address issues, not personalities.
- Focus on what is right, rather than who is wrong.
- No matters should be raised or mentioned that are within the proper remit of a management team meeting.
- During discussions, three minutes is enough time to make a point.
- 'War stories' from the past are not allowed, unless the chairman rules that they are relevant and helpful to the discussion.
- Verbally supported visual presentations should be limited to five minutes.
- Keep to the point – don't be ambiguous or go off the topic being discussed.
- Avoid the use of technical terms others may not understand.
- It is inappropriate to use board meetings to demonstrate superior intellect, knowledge or excellence.
- The chief executive/MD must not inhibit executive directors from expressing alternative views to his or her own.

- When presenting or introducing a topic, assume everyone has read the board papers and never repeat what is in writing.
- Speak slowly and economically – brevity is a virtue.
- During discussions and presentations, listen attentively and display interest in what is being said.
- Be positive and constructive, rather than negative and destructive – only disagree by making a constructive suggestion.

Try getting *your* board to discuss and agree some rules of engagement, circumscribing behaviour that is, and is not, acceptable during board meetings. Produce a preliminary list from ideas solicited from everyone, including some from the list shown above, perhaps. Then have a full discussion and agree a list that everyone subscribes to. Give everyone a copy. You will find that having such a set of rules helps for more effective board meetings and makes your job of chairing them easier too.

An experienced chairman expressed the following views on some of the topics covered in this section

Sir Nigel Mobbs

Our board meetings last from two to three hours. The usual timetable is 10.30 to 12.45. It is the chairman's job to keep an eye on the time. We don't allow OHPs and the like – visual aids tend not to discriminate enough in providing the board with the information it needs. They can present too much information and encourage off-the-cuff talking that can wander from the point. We find it is easier to give everyone a hard copy, which it is assumed has been read beforehand and I encourage people to highlight the salient points, but not to deliver speeches. All the directors have a copy of our 'boardroom conduct' that tells people how they are expected to behave and perform – board meeting etiquette really.

USING COMMITTEES OF THE BOARD

Because boards have a limited amount of time for meetings, committees of the board are often formed to consider certain matters in depth. Such committees are also used to consider matters of a confidential nature. These dedicated committees are sub-groups of the main board that report back to the board with specific recommendations for action.

There is no limitation on what the board can choose to delegate to committees (assuming that the company's Articles of Association permit their formation), but the board must take responsibility for the committees' actions and retain full decision making powers within the board. However, in the case of publicly quoted companies in the UK, the *Combined Code* requires the establishment of nomination, remuneration and audit committees and gives comprehensive guidance on duties and compliance.

The advantages and disadvantages of setting up committees are summarized below.

Advantages:

- allows time to focus on a specific issue;
- builds up more specialized activity and capability in the board;
- reduces burden on board meetings;
- assists decision making – by overcoming board deadlocks and by providing more time and focus for considering decisions;
- may avoid disagreement on the main board;
- useful for sensitive or confidential activities;
- allows non-executive directors to operate in a supervisory role, away from executive directors, but under the board's control.

Disadvantages:

- more directors' time needed – committee attendance additional to board attendance;
- may distance committee activities from board activities;
- increases reporting and coordination tasks;

- can make some executive directors feel left out or 'second-class' board members.

Setting up a committee

When considering the mechanics of setting up a committee, you should remember that different committees play different, and specific, roles. This enables their activities, membership and overall value to the board and to the business to be relatively focused. A committee with a broad or poorly drawn remit of responsibilities can have two major disadvantages: it may not deliver useful outputs because of its lack of focus and it may develop into an alternative or competing 'board'.

In addition, in smaller companies the creation of several committees can be a major investment of time and resource. The values and benefits of establishing committees need to be very carefully considered. There is little point in creating an elaborate board structure including committees, if it produces little of real value and the set-up costs are high. So you should undertake a careful cost–benefit analysis before establishing any committees. To do this, the following questions need to be considered:

- What is the value of setting up the committee?
- What is the role of the committee, for the board and for the company?
- Who should be on the committee?
- What should be its terms of reference?
- What should it produce or deliver?
- To whom, and how, should it report its activities?
- Should the committee have an 'expiry date' or 'review-by date'?

Topics for board committees

The most common committees cover audit, remuneration and nomination, which are referred to briefly below. The *Combined Code*, referred to in Appendix 2, gives comprehensive guidance on these committees. However, committees of the board may be set up to deal with any topic the board decides, such as planning, investments, human resources, donations, health and safety, environmental pollution, risk management, intellectual property and public relations.

Audit committee

The audit committee is an important committee for companies of any size. It will usually have quite wide-ranging powers, including the ability to seek independent professional advice. Its main purpose is to provide a check on both the company's financial controls and auditing processes.

Remuneration committee

This committee recommends the pay and other rewards for executive directors and, often, senior managers. It almost always comprises non-executive directors exclusively, so avoiding the executive directors being involved in determining each other's salaries, bonuses, pensions, share options, service contract terms, etc.

Nomination committee

The purpose of the nomination committee is to vet and recommend potential directors. This approach generally leads to a better, more objectively chosen standard of nomination to the board, which is seen to eliminate favouritism.

Experienced chairmen expressed the following views on some of the topics covered in this section

Sir Nigel Mobbs

My advice about board committees is don't have too many of them – directors are usually quite busy enough. Of course, quoted companies will have to establish audit, remuneration and nomination committees, and a particular business may justify having a specific committee of the board. However, it is best to have board committees as and when they are needed, rather than see them as permanent fixtures. In any case, they should not be a substitute for management and should never make decisions – the board is always the decider.

Dennis Woods

We don't make a great use of board committees. We have set up committees looking at such things as information technology development for the business, and health and safety. These committees are run by management below director level and then advise the board where necessary.

Linda Smith

We have various sub-committees – an audit committee, an employment and remuneration committee, and we also have a particular non-executive director who looks at matters of clinical governance. We are setting up a risk management committee reporting to the board, to look at areas of risk as a whole, including financial risk and clinical risk, so that we can give more time to that. Compliance is an issue for us because we must ensure compliance with all sorts of statutory edicts, rules and regulations, of which there are very many. We are reliant here on a very good board secretary and the directors themselves, who will ensure that things are brought to our attention where we do need to be compliant and to make sure that there are proper ways of being compliant.

CHAPTER CHECKLIST

Here are some questions you might ask yourself in connection with the matters covered in this chapter before you plan any consequent action:

- If many of your board meetings last longer than four hours, do you plan to shorten them by addressing the issues listed on page 116?
- Do you ensure that agendas include all the issues that the board should properly consider, at an appropriate time in the calendar?
- Do you take the necessary time to form preliminary opinions on

all major issues likely to be considered at a meeting in preparing the agenda?

- Are agendas for your board meetings clearly structured, so that directors can understand what is expected for each item?
- Is the shape of the table used for your board meetings conducive to a climate of cohesion rather than separation?
- ... and large enough to give everyone adequate room?
- Do you determine who sits where at board meetings to avoid power groups and to create a sense of cohesion?
- Do you ensure that all aspects of the physical environment in which board meetings take place are really conducive to the high levels of concentration required of the directors?
- Are you making full use of the services that your company secretary can provide to help you with the smooth management of the board's affairs?
- Do you insist that all the information relating to a board meeting is always available to directors at least five days beforehand?
- Has your board agreed some 'rules of presentation' relating to information for board meetings, which everyone abides by?
- When conducting board meetings, do you lead and guide, keeping your views largely to yourself and always display respect, courtesy, patience, humour, goodwill, and the ability to listen well?
- Do you maintain good personal relationships with each director, involving an ongoing dialogue about board issues?
- Are you seen to have a real commitment to the board as a whole and to its objectives, treating all directors in an even-handed way?
- Do you make a point of arriving early for board meetings and ensuring that they start promptly?
- ... in a businesslike way by showing strength and confidence, clarifying what needs to be achieved and when?

- Do you guide the meetings through the agenda items, keeping control of discussions so that they are open and focused, with good communication between directors?
- ... and are all directors encouraged to make appropriate contributions, so tapping into the full range of opinion, knowledge and experience around the board table, to help the best decisions to be made?
- Are you skilful in drawing together the relevant matters from a discussion in a timely way and where appropriate, arriving at a decision that has consensus?
- Do you keep the meetings moving forward at a steady pace and usually finish on time?
- Has your board agreed some 'rules of engagement' that circumscribe behaviour, which everyone adheres to during board meetings?
- Have you considered how committees of the board might improve your board's work?

7

Managing board relationships

CREDIBILITY, PERSONALITIES, POWER AND POLITICS

Encouraging productive relationships

One of your most important responsibilities as chairman of the board is to ensure that the board operates as an effective, dynamic decision making team. To exercise this responsibility you must pay proper regard to a number of issues. One is to have a collection of able and appropriately minded people appointed in the first place – 'you can't make a silk purse from a sow's ear'. Another is to do what you can to ensure that they come together in some sort of unity, where their personalities, energies, motivations, intellects, creativity and wisdom combine in synergy rather than divide in dissipation.

A key to success in this area lies in the relationships that exist between the individuals concerned and how these relationships are nurtured. That is not to say that all the directors must have close and friendly bonds with one another – that is quite unlikely to happen universally, even though some colleagues may well become good friends. However, one would wish to see directors on the same board having a regard for one another that is based on respect, credibility and the give and take of mutual support and common purpose.

The modern chairman takes an active, though often quite subtle role in encouraging the fostering of productive relationships among his or her board colleagues and it is easy to see why. It is that such good relationships are the glue that holds the team together and will encourage directors to challenge one another in a productive way without threat or fear. They encourage those concerned to accept more easily the foibles, weaknesses and strengths of one another, and even private agendas, in a balanced way – so long as there is mutual respect and credibility.

Your function of giving encouragement in these circumstances can be performed in a number of ways. The tenor and climate of your board meetings will be a factor that governs how the directors' relationships and attitudes to one another manifest themselves. Your leadership style and personality at these meetings can help to provide an environment that is open, good-humoured, friendly and unthreatening, despite the need for an appropriate degree of formality.

Away from board meetings you should make sure that you frequently spend some time with each director. Use these opportunities to encourage them to work on their relationships with their colleagues, while cementing your own relationship as part of the same overall process. At the same time, you can engage in some subtle coaching to encourage behaviour that you know will be likely to raise the director's credibility and respect in the eyes of his or her colleagues. You can also discourage any patterns of behaviour that you have observed that are unhelpful to board cohesion and might create negative responses from fellow directors. If you carry out an annual performance appraisal of each director – which I would encourage you to do – you can ensure that matters of relationship building and personal behaviour are topics that are discussed and seen to be important in the context of director performance.

Another good method of helping board members to build better relationships with one another is to organize events where they can spend time together outside board meetings, preferably all together. They could be 'away-days' to brainstorm and think through the strategic options for the company in the years ahead, with a social element too. These events should ideally have a common purpose, but even a social or sporting event can work well.

Power and personalities

The board of directors is accorded a great deal of power – from the shareholders; from society; through the companies acts; through its responsibility for the affairs of the organization and the consequent acquiescence of the employees and the relationships with customers and suppliers. The handling and application of that power are of vital importance to the proper functioning of the board and the health and prosperity of the company. As the board's chairman, you have a crucial role to play in how most of this power is directed and used, and whether it is misused. You must ascertain that no director is exploiting his or her authority as a board member to create personal power bases or to gain favours. In this context it is important that neither you nor the chief executive appear to be behaving in this way.

A board provides an essential mechanism for gaining a consensus view and should derive its strength from the collective, collegiate responsibility of its members. This implies a high degree of harmony, but with an acceptance that disagreements and differences of opinion are healthy features of an effective board, where strong views can be expressed without rancour. While the board's decisions may be influenced by the views of sectional interests, they should not be overshadowed by them or made conditional upon them. In this arrangement there is no hierarchy of power or authority, although the chairman has a clear mandate to lead and manage the board. Similarly, and particularly outside the board itself, the chief executive/MD has clear authority at the head of the company and in the conduct of its everyday business.

Remember that people tend to behave differently when they are members of a group at a meeting, compared with their conduct when interacting singly. As a group, members may tend to disassociate themselves from the topic being considered, or the practical implications, and prefer levels of abstraction. Some can drop out of the discussion altogether because they feel out of their depth. Sometimes the group will tend to avoid the substantive task before it and address the incidental matter instead – such as criticizing the way in which a presentation is made instead of discussing what is being presented. On other occasions the board may try to reach a conclusion based on the lowest common denominator. This can happen when pressure is felt for a conclusion to be made, implying that division must be avoided at all costs. The resultant decision will probably not be the right one, but nobody's ego will have been bruised and compromise has ensured that no positions have been conceded. On the other hand, there is evidence that a group of people may come to riskier decisions than any of the individuals would independently. Research by Kogan and Wallach identified that decisions by individuals on their own are more conservative than those made by the individuals when acting together, because of the diffusion of responsibility in the group. As chairman, you should be aware of these behaviour patterns and take them into account in your handling of the board and the individuals who comprise it.

Ideally, the board should acquire a collective personality, to which all its members must subscribe. However, a group of people coming together in this way will inevitably create a political landscape, where personal agendas encompassing egotism, greed, and the appetite for power, status, advancement and personal favour can provide strong eddy currents and waves that can deflect the board from its proper function. To some degree these issues can always be present – we all have motivations of our own that go beyond fraternity and serving the common good. Difficulties come to the surface when these motivations take precedence or when there are clashes between people because one of them wishes to gain the upper hand. You have to find out about these personal agendas among your board colleagues and try to keep them from disrupting the work of the board and the company.

It is useful for the chairman to have an understanding of the personalities and characters of his or her fellow directors and some insights into their behaviour and motivations. You may pose the question, 'Is everyone really pulling their full weight as a director and adding value to the board's work?' If the answer in some cases is negative, you could well explore why that is and think of ways in which you might act as a catalyst for improvement. There is often an issue of insecurity, or timidity, or the fear of reprisal. At the other end of the scale are those who sometimes appear superior, unaccommodating or thick skinned. In other cases, particularly with those who are new to directing, it could be a case of not being sure what is expected of them, or inexperience.

It may help you in gaining some of these insights if you consider the personal characteristics of each director, using the list displayed in the first section of Chapter 5. Look out too for the way these individuals behave during discussions at board meetings. Some may tend to adopt an adversarial style, while others may tend to default to a more subjective or passive mode. The most common adversarial styles are:

- *Egotistical* – criticism of an idea is seen as an attack on the person holding it. 'Debate' is used to score points against others. 'Logic' is used to reinforce emotion. Opinion poses as evidence.
- *Rigid* – thinking is limited to propositions about perceived reality. The exploration of facts is denied. Propositions made by others that are outside the limits of the rigid thinker are dismissed as irrelevant.
- *Political* – obtaining results or favour is perceived as being achieved by alignment with the ideas of those promoting them. Propositions are attacked or defended, rather than explored. Effort is dissipated in creating power bases, undermining opponents, conniving, rumour-mongering and manipulating others.

Most of the time, the different views of the directors expressed at board meetings will be resolved by a consensus agreement being reached. Such agreement usually requires a degree of accommodation, collaboration and compromise to resolve any real or potential conflict. The various styles that people adopt when faced with views that conflict with their own are shown in Figure 7.1. Clearly, if you have a highly political board where people are prone to pursuing their own goals, your skills and patience when chairing meetings could be severely tested. On the other hand, non-assertive or passive board members who are also uncooperative will often tend to avoid conflict altogether and try to deny its existence. This too is an unsatisfactory situation. The resolution of conflict requires interaction that is mutually reciprocal – ie the style adopted by one person or group will affect the style adopted by the other.

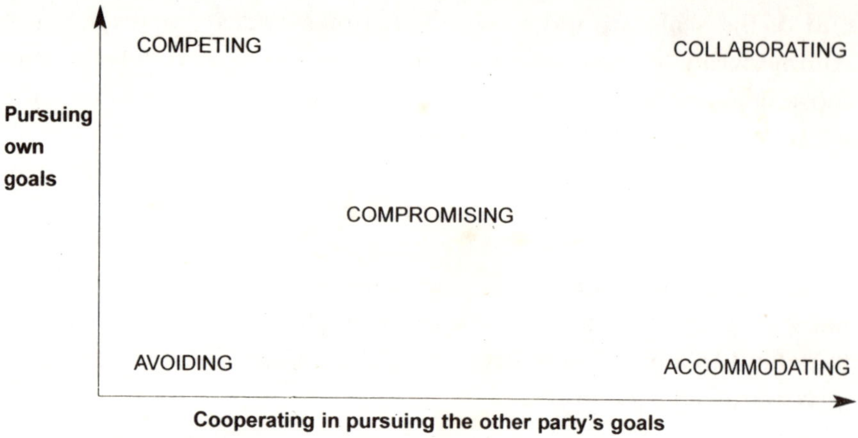

Figure 7.1 Domain of consensus and conflict

Coaching and supporting

One of your many roles as chairman of the board is to act as a coach and supporter to the individual directors and to the whole group. Some people have a natural gift for this kind of work and you may well be one of them. However, everyone can learn new skills, concepts and tips to help carry out this role to the best of their potential. To this end, you may find a book by Kalinauckas and King, *Coaching: Realising the potential* (1994) helpful. It is written for quite a wide audience but you will doubtless find much of the contents applicable to your needs in relation to the board and its members. Here is a small (adapted) extract from the book on coaching at meetings, which you may find useful:

> *Focus on how you can coach participants to make decisions and commit to action. Ask yourself, 'How can I coach these people effectively to move this meeting on?' Take time to listen carefully to the conversations and the way people are talking. Is the discussion short, sharp and to the point or is it more relaxed and open? Get a sense of the speed and tone of voice and gradually tune yourself into the conversation. On a corner of your meeting pad draw two lines crossing each other, one horizontal and the other vertical. Write 'problems' on the left of the horizontal line and 'opportunities' on the right. Write 'future' at the top of the vertical line and 'past' at the bottom. Make a mark in the four quarters of the cross indicating whether the different parts of the conversation are about the past or the future, are they opportunities or problems.*

See how you can now move the conversations more into the top right hand corner by talking about how things could be in the future. The kind of questions you can ask are:

- How could we achieve that?
- What can be done to make further improvements?
- Who else can we bring on board to help?
- How can we make things better?
- What are we looking to do to move things forward?
- What are we trying to achieve?
- How would that help us?

Induction and inclusion

Newly appointed executive and non-executive directors should spend time with the chairman as part of a properly arranged induction programme. A similar procedure can apply in both cases, except that the non-executive director must also have some planned periods to see the facilities and employees of the business at first hand and to spend time with the executive directors to understand their work. During the first six months or so of an executive director's appointment, executive duties will inevitably place a premium on his or her time. For this reason alone, it is important that the chairman sets aside a series of short, well-planned, productive meetings with the director during this period, to help ensure that he or she becomes an effective, well-informed board member as well.

A proper induction is essential for all new directors if they are to play their proper role within a reasonably short timescale. An executive director will need to become familiar with his or her particular executive role in the company, but all directors should learn about how the company is managed generally and, in particular, how it relates to its customers, suppliers and employees and how the last of these are organized and motivated. Just as important is an induction by the chairman into the board's affairs, the style of the board, how issues are dealt with both inside and outside the boardroom and the way that reports and information are best presented. A sketch of each board member can be useful, covering their personalities and each of their special strengths and experience. The chairman can also explain, in the same context, how the new director can best help with board balance, and also how he or she can help the chairman in carrying out the tasks of leading the board and managing its business. The appointee can also be familiarized with the important aspects of the company's history, policies and personalities, as well as its culture. The new director must also understand the company's strategic objectives and the main issues that have been absorbing the board's time during the preceding year or so. Awareness of the issues likely to be facing the board in the future will also be important.

Guidance should be given on how best to behave at board meetings and how acceptance and respect may be earned. This aspect is of particular relevance since, unless the new director is felt to be a worthy colleague by his or her peers, he or she will not become included as an accepted and respected member of the board. Unless this state of affairs is achieved within the first three months or so, it will often become an increasingly steep hill to climb and may result in the appointment being a complete failure.

The company secretary can also play a useful part in this initiation process, since he or she serves the board and its members in many ways. For example, new directors would do well to familiarize themselves with the company's Memorandum and Articles of Association, where the company secretary can act as a useful guide.

Induction and inclusion checklist

At a minimum, these topics should be covered in the process:

- how the company is managed generally;
- how the company relates to its principal stakeholders;
- how the employees are organized and motivated;
- the style of the board;
- how board issues are dealt with;
- the presentation of board information and reports;
- personalities, strengths and experience of each director;
- appointee's strengths relative to board balance;
- how the appointee can give support to the chairman;
- the company's history, personalities, culture and policies;

- strategic objectives of the company;
- main board issues over the past year or so;
- issues likely to face the board;
- recommended behaviour at board meetings and elsewhere;
- the company's Memorandum and Articles of Association.

Experienced chairmen expressed the following views on some of the topics covered in this section

Sir Nigel Mobbs

A balanced board needs a fair degree of compatibility among the directors, based largely on mutual respect. That means respecting the opinions of others and being open to different opinions, but accepting when you are a minority and being big enough to say you won't object. Then, once the board has made a decision, being supportive of that decision, regardless of personal views held and expressed, even where an opposite point of view had been put very forcibly beforehand. The chairman must create an environment where such differences of opinion can be aired and discussed without rancour, which is why compatibility is so important. A bad egg can be very disruptive.

Having the right board is a key factor in the handling of personalities and politics. You then have to understand where people are coming from, but there is no easy way of handling personalities, particularly if they are too big and lack compatibility with others. There may be a risk that some heavyweight non-executive directors try to hunt the executives aggressively. If so, the chairman should have a word in their ear, advising that executive directors may respect their wisdom but that they dislike their criticism, which they feel is all the time sniping. A very wise chairman once advised me when I joined his board as a non-executive director not to say anything for the first three meetings. He explained that it is sensible to wait and see how the board culture works in practice and so avoid creating a revolution on day one. I would give the same advice to executive directors too, particularly not to speak on things they don't know about.

Dennis Woods

To handle personalities and politics at board level you have to understand the makeup of each person and relate to them accordingly. I know that I must play to everyone's strengths and recognize, even compensate for, weaknesses. If I have any concerns about personal agendas I find it is best to raise issues when they occur or when it is appropriate to do so. We can have some quite heated discussions on such matters. It does help me to understand personal agendas and where people are coming from.

Michael Mander

I feel very strongly that every director has a duty to serve all the shareholders and not act as a delegate of a particular interest, even though he or she may be there because a particular shareholder has asked that they be appointed. Their job as a director is to put the company first, so representing the interests of all the shareholders. Where there are a small number of shareholders that are all 'represented' on the board, it is vital that the chairman is, and is seen to be, even-handed on board matters. At the same time, one must not become a nut between two or more crackers. I find that I can strike that difficult balancing act because of the directors' perception of my integrity – all parties must respect the chairman. Where the balance can become difficult is between standing back enough so that you are not taking sides on issues, but on the other hand, not evading your responsibility by stepping back too far. And if you think someone is behaving badly, you can't just let it pass – so it is quite a delicate tightrope on occasion. Above all in these circumstances, it is important not to let board meetings slip into shareholders' meetings.

Linda Smith

I suppose my own philosophy and approach is that the chair needs to make the board warm and personally supportive enough so that it can be intellectually really quite aggressive at times. The personal relationships and the respect people have for each other and the way that we work together, allows there to be some real, hard-hitting challenge over issues. You can only do that if people aren't too sensitive and don't feel personally threatened, so it is important to get that balance right. I would say the big part of my day-to-day role is making sure that it feels a place where people feel comfortable making their contribution. They should feel that they can say, 'I totally disagree with that' and, 'I really want to ask you why you think that would work' or, 'I'm not sure that's the way we should be going.'

Although the chair sets the tone and style of the board in some ways, I think you have to be prepared to do it in your own way. I'm me and I couldn't carry on for eight years being something I wasn't. I am a friendly person, I'm not reserved, I don't throw authority around – I think it has to be earned, I'm a relationship builder.

The chair and the chief executive have to work to provide the political space, in what is a very politicized service, to allow us sometimes to kick against the traces and set our own priorities. To do this, we have to have a reputation of being straight, committed, balanced, financially careful and a good service provider.

I did feel that things weren't changing fast enough and I had a crisis of confidence when the government was about to change, when my overriding concern was around the issue of organizational capability, that was one thing that in a sense I couldn't do. I didn't think the organization was changing and I didn't think that the chief executive paid attention to it, and so I had to say so. We discussed the matter together and we got some help with organizational development, we got him a mentor to help him with managing the changes and the relationships with his fellow executives.

That was a very difficult, challenging period. All the executive directors, including the chief executive, had to reapply for their jobs. They had been a management team for a long time – too long in my view – there had been no breath of change and they were far too cosy. As a result of this reorganization, two of the executive directors had to be made redundant

> and the chief executive did it, and believed in doing it. The new directors, appointed to replace them, but in different, new roles, are a breath of fresh air and the whole feel of the board as well as its dynamic have changed. The chief executive and I worked together on these changes and I saw my role as being sometimes pushing and sometimes supporting.

WORKING WITH THE CHIEF EXECUTIVE OR MANAGING DIRECTOR

A strong alliance

The roles of the chairman and the chief executive/MD are distinct and separate, although complementary. Ideally, they benefit from being filled by people with different personalities and motivations, each particularly suited to the role concerned. While the chief executive/MD would probably be thrusting, energetic and essentially focused on results, the chairman needs to be more reflective, politically astute and focused on the longer term. Whatever the reality of the situation in which they may find themselves, the two individuals should constitute a strong, mutually supportive alliance at the head of the company, who complement one another and don't get in each other's way. Moreover, it is important that everyone, both inside and outside the organization, can see that this is a reality. Nowhere is this more necessary than with the directors, where the complementary nature of the relationship, or lack of it, will be most keenly felt.

While it is important for the chairman to have a good working relationship with each director, the rapport with the chief executive/MD is crucial. The key here is to be sure to have frequent and regular sessions together, even though many of them may be quite short. This is where problems and new ideas can be shared at an early stage, encouragement given and caution advocated. They can also provide opportunities for the chairman to gain an understanding of how each of the executive directors is performing in their roles as managers. Given the likely pressures and commitments facing the chief executive/MD, the chairman will probably have to go the extra mile to keep this relationship as it should be, but that added effort will be well rewarded.

Deciding who does what

When one encounters differences and tensions that have arisen between the chairman and the chief executive/MD on a board, the problem frequently has at its heart the issue of who does what. Resolving and clarifying the answer to that question cannot only make both of them much more effective in their respective roles, but the synergy created has an additional positive effect on the board and the whole organization. Even where such tensions have not become a significant problem, a reappraisal of who does what can often be a worthwhile exercise, particularly when the situation of the organization or one of the individuals concerned has changed. Central to an agreement about the tasks that will be performed by both parties is an understanding by them both of what each role entails. The following are the suggested essential tasks of the chairman of the board and of the chief executive/MD respectively.

Essential tasks of the chairman:

- providing leadership to the board;
- taking responsibility for the board's composition and development;
- ensuring proper information for the board;
- planning and conducting board meetings effectively;
- getting all the directors involved in the board's work;
- ensuring the board focuses on its key tasks;
- engaging the board in assessing and improving its performance;
- overseeing the induction and development of directors;
- supporting the chief executive/MD.

Essential tasks of the chief executive/MD:

- developing strategic operating plans that reflect the longer-term corporate objectives and priorities established by the board;
- maintaining an ongoing dialogue with the chairman of the board;

- playing a full part in the work of the board and encouraging executive directors to do so;
- maintaining the business portfolio in line with the board's decisions;
- delivering the operational performance of the company;
- ensuring that adequate operational planning and financial control systems are in place;
- providing leadership to management and other employees;
- ensuring that the operating objectives, policies and standards of performance are not only understood but owned and followed by the management and other employees;
- closely monitoring the operating and financial results against plans and budgets;
- taking remedial action where necessary and informing the board of significant changes;
- managing the company day to day.

If you and your chief executive/MD agree to undertake such a review, it may prove useful to discuss and elaborate upon these lists of tasks as a first step. In doing so, be sure to discuss not only the scope of what each task entails but, particularly, where areas of overlap and interface with the tasks of the other person could occur and the consequent implications. Look out, too, to highlight areas where one person could give support to the other. Remember to consider also the areas external to the company where either of you might play a role in representing the company. It may be helpful to use the following checklist to facilitate this process.

Checklist of essential tasks

	Chairman	CE/MD
1. Ensuring that the board develops a vision of the future.		
2. Ensuring that aims, objectives, missions and strategies are established.		
3. Developing and preparing strategic plans.		
4. Ensuring that the board lays down policies and overall priorities.		

	Chairman	CE/MD
5. The establishment and maintenance of values and culture.		
6. Ensuring that the board monitors performance against strategies / plans.		
7. Execution of strategies, plans and policies.		
8. Ensuring that company reputation and achievements are protected.		
9. Planning and running board meetings.		
10. Developing the board to work as a team.		
11. Ensuring that top managers have space to perform.		
12. Representing the company to shareholders.		
13. Representing the company to other stakeholders.		
14. Effectively communicating policies to employees.		
15. Adherence to laws and regulations.		
16. Ensuring customers' needs are part of the board's business.		
17. Ensuring employees' commitment and concerns are part of the board's business.		
18. Securing the confidence and support of the directors.		
19. Ensuring that all the directors contribute to the board's work.		
20. Setting the style, tone and tempo of the board.		
21. Leading the employees.		
22. The management of risk and reputation.		

The idea is to develop a partnership approach, where you play to one another's strengths and each supports the other, particularly in areas of relative weakness. Having an unambiguous understanding of the two distinct roles and how they can interlock and complement each other is a vital foundation for such a dynamic duo.

Experienced chairmen expressed the following views on some of the topics covered in this section

Sir Nigel Mobbs

Working with the chief executive/MD is largely a matter of the 'chemistry' between them. Clearly a chairman has to be sensitive to the strengths and weaknesses of his or her colleague and provide some sort of supplementary support where weaknesses do exist, and where appropriate. This can be done by either encouraging greater dependence on one of the other executive directors (eg finance), or, indeed, for the chairman to fill some of the gaps, depending on what they are. On the other hand, if the chief executive/MD is over-strong, the chairman's role may be to act as something of a brake and a voice for reason. Indeed, this may also be needed when there are weak areas. The chairman has to adopt quite a sensitive position to make sure that he or she doesn't allow any lack of self-confidence of the chief executive/MD to get in the way of achievement, while also making sure that enthusiasm isn't dampened. Sometimes the chief executive/MD can fill in and support any weaknesses that the chairman may have – this is where they must work it out between them. But it is more important that the chairman understands the chief executive's strengths and weaknesses than for the chief executive/MD to try filling the chairman's role. If that happens, one can get into the dilemmas caused by too much power and authority being executed by one person, which could be a slippery slope. Interestingly, the corporate governance argument hasn't addressed the case where a strong and dominant chief executive/MD might try to ensure the appointment of a weak chairman to protect his or her own position.

Linda Smith

I think the chair and the chief executive are the two most important board roles and there have been lots of breakdowns in the health service between the two holders. My own view is that that is because there hasn't been absolutely clear and transparent discussion about where the boundaries between the two roles are. They need to have a relationship where they can sit down together and discuss exactly what the two roles are and where the boundary is, and work at it with good humour and respect over a long period. They also need to explore what things they can powerfully do together, where they can be complementary and where they can be partners and develop these.

My chief executive and I work well together. The fact that we respect one another helps, but the relationship is not without its tensions, which we recognize are there and are necessary. These tensions are not destructive but could become so if we couldn't discuss it. I think that is the key relationship, which works with the right degree of informality, where it's all right to challenge and use a bit of humour – it's a dynamic relationship.

COMBINING THE ROLES OF CHAIRMAN AND CHIEF EXECUTIVE/MD

The *Combined Code on Corporate Governance* calls for a separate chairman and chief executive/MD at the head of a company whose shares are traded on the London Stock Exchange. This requirement stems from the need for shareholders to feel assured that too much power is not in the hands of one person and followed some earlier well-publicized cases of the misuse of power. This is what the *Code* says on the subject:

> *There should be a clear division of responsibilities at the head of the company between the running of the board and the executive responsibility for the running of the company's business. No one individual should have unfettered powers of decision.*

Despite the undoubted advantages of having two separate people fulfilling the roles of chairman and chief executive/MD, there are many companies where it is not appropriate or practicable to do so. Indeed, most private companies, perhaps because of their relatively small size, have one person at the head of the organization who acts in both these roles. If you find yourself in the position of having to combine these two roles, it is helpful to consider the potential shortcomings of doing so and what might be done to mitigate them.

An obvious disadvantage, from what has been said in the previous section, is that the benefits of a synergistic partnership of mutually supportive characters, each playing to his or her strengths and buttressing the weaknesses of the other, are not realized. One of the intrinsic advantages of such an alliance is that sensitive problems can sometimes be shared and the interaction between the two minds can often lead to creative but practical solutions. The temperament and motivations of most people who combine the two roles would be biased towards those most suitable for fulfilling the chief executive's role. After all, the pressure for immediate results and the need for energy and drive to lead and sustain the business are realities for most companies, particularly smaller ones. Some people are fortunate in having the personal qualities to succeed as a chief executive/MD combined with those requiring a more reflective, longer-term focus. However, most will find the chairman role being very much in second place, crowded out for the most part by the demands and satisfaction of 'making it happen'. And when the pressure is on, management demands will inevitably take precedence over those of governance.

Another potential problem area can be a difficulty in getting the board to stand back and be really objective about the performance of the management, particularly in the achievement of strategic goals. This is especially true when the board is all-executive and effectively *is* the management. Because most of the interaction between the leader and the executive directors will be in management mode, it is sometimes difficult for the latter to see the need to change roles. Indeed, the combined roles of the leader can often make it more difficult for executive directors to act in their director roles.

Part of the answer is to clearly separate management meetings from board meetings and their agendas. Having these two types of meeting on different days, and even at different frequencies too, can help here. It is also vital for the leader to unequivocally separate the chairman role from that of chief executive/MD and to make it clear to his or her colleagues which mode he or she is in, particularly when at meetings. This can be reinforced by the act of ruling out executive matters that may be raised at board meetings and putting them on the agenda of the next management meeting, where that is appropriate. Conversely, if the consequence of a decision made at a management meeting is clearly a matter for the board to consider, making a point of that and referring it to the next board meeting will help to clarify the two distinct roles to all concerned.

The fact that one person is more vulnerable than two presents another obvious quandary that needs to be resolved. It is not always possible to have a competent successor waiting in the wings but it is clear that attention should be paid to succession planning, where it is feasible. Perhaps the most pragmatic solution would be the appointment of a deputy chairman, who could chair the board in the event of serious illness or death and take the initiative to find a new leader. This arrangement calls for the appointment of a non-executive director with appropriate qualities and experience.

At the same time, appointing an operations director can help create more time for the chairman role.

As a more general consideration, having a small cadre of high-calibre non-executive directors with extensive board experience on the board can undoubtedly help to overcome many of the shortcomings of having one person occupying both of these important posts.

Experienced chairmen expressed the following views on some of the topics covered in this section

Michael Mander

I think combining the roles of chairman and chief executive/MD has worked well when the company is small, but there comes a point when there should be a split of roles. The criteria for when that split should take place will usually concern the size and complexity of the company. I buy the concept completely of having separate chairmen and chief executives/MDs, as opposed to the US system. But combining them serves young companies particularly well, usually with a small board too.

Sir Nigel Mobbs

I am not hostile to the idea of one person taking the roles of both chairman and chief executive/MD, but in a perfect world I think separating them is sensible. If they are combined, you definitely need to have one of the non-executive directors as a 'lead director' who can stand up to the person who is chairman and chief executive if necessary. But there are situations where it is crazy not to have one person in both roles, such as in times of major change. For example, when a chief executive/MD has failed and leaves the company, it is best for the chairman to take on both roles and have all the strings in his or her hand until a new chief executive/MD is appointed. Also, there are types of business, and particularly in some small companies, where perhaps the skill and talent of the one person is such that splitting the roles might damage the business, at least temporarily. There are also times when the separation of the roles can create conflict, if the relationship is not good. Essentially, conflict can be avoided or reduced if the responsibilities of the two separate people and roles can be clearly mapped out, identifying who does what. When drawing up the lists, one can try to play to the strengths of either party. In the broadest terms, the chairman's role is focused on strategy creation and agreeing the way forward and it is the key task of the chief executive/MD to implement it.

WORKING WITH THE NON-EXECUTIVE DIRECTORS

There is no doubt that well-selected non-executive directors can add enormously to the quality of a board's decisions and its overall effectiveness. This increases the chances of the company acting in the best interests of its long-term security and prosperity. The introduction of truly independent judgement to the board's activities provides greater assurance that the correct strategies and decisions are likely to be chosen. The non-executive directors can also help to raise the calibre and competence of the board and, in so doing, the ability of the company to play in a different league. Securing the right people to serve on the board in this role is an essential first step, and was touched on in Chapter 5. However, it is vitally important to get the most from them throughout the lifetime of their appointments in respect of their potential to add value to the board's work and to the company, in a number of ways.

Personal counsel

Many chairmen use their non-executive directors to provide general counsel and a different perspective on matters of concern. They also seek their guidance on particular issues before they are raised at board meetings. Some see a respected non-executive director as a source of trusted objective criticism that may not be welcome from other sources.

Strategic direction

As 'outsiders', the non-executive directors should have a clearer or wider view of external factors affecting the company and its business environment than the executive directors. The normal role of the non-executive director in strategy formation is therefore to provide a creative and informed contribution and to act as a constructive, objective critic in looking at the plans devised by the executive team.

Performance

One of the essential tasks of non-executive directors is to scrutinize the performance of management in meeting agreed goals and objectives and monitor the reporting of performance. In doing so, care must be taken to avoid being seen largely as 'policemen' by the executives and this requires a positive, businesslike approach that is seen to be supportive and undertaken in the best interests of the organization.

Troubleshooting

In times of crisis, occasions can arise when only the non-executive directors are capable of acting on behalf of the company. This is especially true if a business has been badly managed and the chief executive/MD needs to be replaced. It would be very difficult for the executive directors to take a lead at board level in these circumstances; non-executive directors have to take the initiative for the whole board.

Connections

The company's and board's effectiveness can often benefit from outside contacts and opinions. An important function for non-executive directors, therefore, can be to help connect the business and board with networks of potentially useful people and organizations. In some cases, the non-executive directors may be called upon to represent the company externally.

Board committees

Some of the main specialist roles of non-executive directors will often be carried out in a board committee. The board's ability to operate efficiently is often increased by the establishment of committees to give more detailed and objective consideration to major issues before they are formally discussed at the board. While the number and types of board committee vary from company to company, the key responsibilities of non-executive directors serving on them show some consistency. The main areas are as follows.

Audit

It is the duty of the whole board to ensure that the company accounts properly to its shareholders by presenting a true and fair reflection of its actions and financial performance and that the necessary internal control systems are put into place and monitored regularly and rigorously. Non-executive directors have an important part to play in fulfilling this responsibility, whether or not a formal audit committee (composed of non-executive directors) of the board has been constituted.

Remuneration of executive directors

Devising the appropriate remuneration packages for the executive directors can be one of the most contentious issues a board faces – even in private companies. This contention is reduced if decisions on executive salary, bonuses and other benefits are seen to be made by those who do not stand to gain directly and are independent from the management. In listed companies and some larger private companies, therefore, policy on executive remuneration is usually devised by a committee of non-executive directors.

Appointments to the board

One of the board's most crucial functions is to decide on new appointments to the board and to approve other senior appointments in the company. Again, in some cases, much of the work is done by a committee, where non-executive directors usually play an important part.

This can be particularly apposite where objective advice on succession is required, especially where the chairman or chief executive/MD is concerned.

The exact role and contribution of non-executive directors can appear hard to define. In large part this stems from the myriad reasons for a board of directors choosing to make a particular appointment. In addition, existing directors may have different expectations of the role from shareholders and other interested parties. Perhaps an important consideration from the executive directors' perspective is for them to have non-executive colleagues that they believe can be useful to them. The board should be considered as a team, with the independent non-executive directors as members of that team. Hopefully the appointments will have been made with the balance of that team in mind, with a fit in terms of complementary skills, experience and personalities.

The breadth of experience of the non-executive directors is an important factor here. One aspect of this derives from the rich variety of circumstances they will probably have faced collectively as members of diverse boards. In these many situations they would have been party to hosts of discussions, examining facts, opinions, information and misinformation, considering risk and potential reward. They would also have seen how different boards, each with a particular constitution, style and personality, approached these various considerations and decisions. Then, with the benefit of hindsight, they will have been able to judge the many approaches in the light of the consequent outcomes. This treasure chest is available for the chairman and the board to draw upon, provided that the circumstances are right. To ensure that this can happen, it is important that the chairman maintains a good working relationship with each of the non-executive directors from the time of their appointment. Another enabling factor will be that the climate at board meetings is conducive to profiting from this knowledge – a situation that the chairman can have a key role in influencing. The principal outcome will be that the board will inevitably come to better quality decisions. Another can be that the executive directors, in their roles as directors, learn and develop from the experience. The guidance given for non-executive directors of publicly quoted companies in the Higgs report is included in Appendix 2 on pages 207–09.

Experienced chairmen expressed the following views on some of the topics covered in this section

Michael Mander

The question of having to handle strong personalities on the board depends crucially on the attitude of those concerned. The chairman must be influential on who is appointed to the board, so hopefully somebody who is destructively strong rather than constructively strong won't be appointed. I know non-executive directors who are forceful in their views – which doesn't mean they talk a lot or hog the discussion – but nobody on the board is in any doubt whatsoever as to what they think about a particular issue. They can express their views in a most robust manner where necessary, without offending anybody, which I think is fine.

One of the unfortunate and unintentional consequences of the Cadbury Report was that it gave a perception that non-executive directors come as a sort of internal vigilante force, as it were. In my view, that is a very small part of their total responsibility and something they would exercise only rarely. I do believe that they are really there to bring the benefits of their experience to the development of the company as a whole and not for disciplinary reasons.

One must guard against non-executive and executive directors becoming 'we' and 'they'. This can happen very easily, I think, particularly with a young company when the executive directors are themselves young and by definition are inexperienced as directors. The non-executive directors can then quite easily be seen as carping and criticizing, rather than trying to draw from their experience, which would make them appear to be in another camp to the executives. Other than in audit committees and the like, I try very hard not to have separate meetings of the non-executive directors, for the reason that I don't want the executive directors to think that we are going into a huddle to talk about something behind their back, as it were. I do try to give my non-executive directors advice and guidance as to traps that they might fall into in this area – things they need to be sensitive to.

One of my jobs between board meetings, as chairman, is to keep the non-executive directors up to date with anything that is important. This includes areas where they may have an input to make and also matters that they should be alerted to or could influence. I sometimes have to warn them not to pile on too much pressure to an executive who might be at full stretch. They will often ring me and say that they feel strongly about an issue and that they wanted to let me know that they intend to raise the matter fairly forcefully at the coming meeting and do I have a problem with that? In response I would normally say that of course I did not, and this approach seems to work very well.

Linda Smith

I try to keep in touch with the non-executive directors by telephone and talk to them informally and to work with them, to make sure they are properly inducted and that they have development. Once a year I assess them and give them an opportunity to talk to me about what I can do differently that will make their role easier to perform, what they think about the way the board is run and different issues. Because I do that often they feel able to say if they are unhappy about something and express what they feel. So it is a fairly free-flowing, ongoing relationship, with a point in the year when we meet to do an assessment. This is a two-way relationship, because I am eager to know what they think about the way I carry out my role. I need to know that and, after all, they are responsible, experienced people so I need to listen to them.

CHAPTER CHECKLIST

Here are some questions you might ask yourself in connection with the matters covered in this chapter before you plan any consequent action:

- Are the relationships between all your directors as they should be?
- … based upon respect, credibility, mutual support and common purpose?

- ... and are you active in encouraging such relationships?
- Do you ensure that the board's power is not misused or misdirected?
- Does your board derive its strength from the collective, collegiate responsibility of its members?
- Are you aware of various collective behaviour patterns that your directors might adopt?
- ... and take them into account when handling the board and individual directors?
- Are you aware of any personal agendas among your colleagues?
- ... and do you keep them from disrupting the board and the company?
- Do you understand the personalities of your fellow directors and have insights into their behaviour and motivations?
- ... and provide support and guidance as a coach?
- Do you put time aside to help with the induction and inclusion of newly-appointed directors?
- ... covering at least the items listed on pages 150–51?
- Are you and your chief executive/MD seen as a strong, mutually supportive alliance?
- ... and do you meet frequently with the chief executive/MD to help make it fruitful?
- Do you and the chief executive/MD periodically review 'who does what' to help minimize conflicts and misunderstandings?
- ... where the checklist on pages 156–57 may prove useful?
- If you are both the chairman and the chief executive/MD, do you overcome most of the shortcomings of combining the roles?
- ... and take practical steps to separate the two roles?
- Have you considered using the non-executive directors on your board more comprehensively?
- ... including drawing fully on their experience?
- ... and do you maintain good relationships with them to enable this to happen?
- ... as well as creating an appropriate climate at board meetings?

8

Assessing and improving effectiveness

ATTRIBUTES OF THE SUCCESSFUL CHAIRMAN

Every chairman will develop a personal style that suits his or her personality and individual strengths and is adapted to the circumstances of any particular board that he or she is serving on. Each will show a high order of skill in many of the important areas that constitute the domain of the modern chairman and some may even be excellent in all of them. However, for most of us, there remain areas that could and must be improved in order to deserve the accolade of comprehensive success. I have therefore attempted to identify those areas and the attributes displayed by chairmen who can address them successfully. Some are *personal characteristics,* others are about where *focus and responsibilities* should lie and some are in particular areas of *skill and competence.*

Personal characteristics

The span of personal characteristics that one would want to see displayed by a board of directors was considered in Chapter 5 and many of them might well be particularly desirable for the chairman to have. Notwithstanding that, if one considers which particular characteristics might be deemed mandatory for a really successful chairman to possess, the list shortens.

Personal integrity would doubtless be the one that heads the shortlist. This characteristic identifies someone who is truthful and trustworthy, can be relied upon to keep his or her word and does not have double standards or compromise on ethical and legal matters. These are qualities that one would hope to find in most directors but are clearly essential for the person who should be seen to lead the board by example.

Another vital personal characteristic is the ability to influence others without domination. This is often associated with confidence and presence, highly developed coordination skills and the subtle use of persuasiveness with sensitivity. Doubtless, anyone who is consistently to realize the full potential of the board needs this ability – autocracy, control and dominance are the antithesis of this.

Decisiveness, with an insistence on getting things done, is another crucial characteristic. If the chairman does not have this attribute, board meetings can become protracted shambles, where issues are talked to death without clear conclusions being reached. Such meetings will lack a sense of purpose and the board would not be truly aware of the objectives that needed to be achieved. Let's face it, an indecisive decision making body is a contradiction in terms.

Although it is the last mentioned here, intellectual capacity could well be regarded as the most important of the personal characteristics referred to. That is not to say that all really successful chairmen will possess a brilliant mind. Rather, it is the capacity for understanding, thinking and reasoning that will mark the people who reach a high level of competence and effectiveness in the chairman's role and differentiate them from the rest.

Focus and responsibilities

Here I am identifying the key areas that the chairman should take personal responsibility for and where his or her expertise must be focused. There is an overarching need for chairmen to acquire the ability to ensure that the board properly addresses all the major strategic issues that will affect the company's viability, reputation and prosperity. This, after all, is 'the bottom line' – it's about realizing the essential purpose for which the board exists. If the chairman cannot make sure that this is achieved then the company will almost certainly founder, given time. However, this composite ability requires competence in a number of vital spheres.

The chairman must have a proper focus on the key tasks that the board must carry out and ensure that they are all addressed effectively. These will include the tasks concerned largely with determining the company's aspirations, values and its interface with other parties and also those tasks concerned with the specific direction in which the company will develop, focused on the setting and achievement of business objectives. These tasks encompass agreeing policies for the organization and the provision of resources.

The success of the board is clearly crucially dependent on the calibre and competence of the individual directors, their overall range of knowledge, skill and experience and how well they come together as an effective working group. Getting all of these aspects right is one of the chairman's essential responsibilities, embracing as it does the board's constitution and development, including matters of succession.

As the board's leader, the chairman needs to have a sense of purpose and an ability to keep a vision of the future for the organization clearly in his or her mind. This constant concern for where the company is heading helps in guiding the board to focus on the strategic objectives that must be achieved and the related priorities.

Another important sphere of responsibility is to engage the board in assessing how it is performing in all the key areas and in the associated processes of continuous learning and improvement. Coupled with this is the need to make a personal commitment to oversee the induction of new appointees to the board and encourage the professional development of individual directors.

Skill and competence

Perhaps the principal attribute under this heading is an ability to plan and manage the board's business well. As we have seen in an earlier chapter, such ability encompasses many areas of knowledge and individual skills and competencies, often significantly influenced by behaviour. They span such issues as getting agendas, the physical environment and information presented for meetings right, to the way meetings are conducted, where the chairman's skills as leader and guide are critically tested.

It is important that the full range of the directors' knowledge, experience, opinion, creativity and questioning skills are brought to bear on the issues facing the board. This is why the chairman's ability to engage all the board members fully and to effectively manage relationships with them are so important. Highly developed political and interpersonal skills are key requirements here.

A good relationship between the chairman and the chief executive/MD is vital to the success of the board and the enterprise as a whole. In handling that relationship, it is usually the chairman who needs to go that extra mile by supporting his or her colleague. Critically, such support will often require skills as mentor, adviser and sounding board, conditioned by mutual respect and trust.

Checklist of attributes displayed by successful contemporary chairmen

Some readers may wish to evaluate their ability against each of the following characteristics, to help identify those areas where personal development might be most beneficial. The checklist summarizes the points raised above and is provided for that purpose. No attempt has been made to give weightings to the characteristics or to rank them:

- Personal integrity and authority, without domination.
- Intellectual capacity.
- Decisiveness and an insistence to get things done.
- Ability to ensure that the board properly addresses all the major strategic issues that will affect the company's prosperity, viability and reputation.
- Having a proper focus on the board's key tasks and ensuring that they are addressed.
- Taking responsibility for the board's constitution and development, including succession matters.
- A sense of purpose, a vision and a set of priorities and objectives, with skill in guiding the board to focus on the relevant issues.

- Engaging the board in assessing and improving its effectiveness.
- Overseeing the induction of new appointees and the development of individual directors.
- Ability in planning and managing the board's business.
- Political skills and an ability to engage all the board members and manage the relationships.
- Acting as an effective mentor, sounding board and adviser to the chief executive/MD (and other directors).

Guidance on the role of the chairman is contained in the Higgs report and is reproduced on pages 206–07 of Appendix 2.

Experienced chairmen expressed the following views on some of the topics covered in this section

Sir Nigel Mobbs

The most important factors in a chairman's success are having the right board and having some good luck too. Being in the right business at the right time is very important, provided you take advantage of it. In most of the successful companies you can point to the chairman having a major influence, providing leadership without being overbearing or oppressive, but with a good board. And getting a good board is part of the job – a team with good structure, disciplines, rules and housekeeping. So you must pick the right people and get round pegs in round holes – people with competence and the right fit for a particular board. Making these judgements is vital, but if you make a mistake, don't blame the misfit!

Linda Smith

Looking at the attributes that I think I need to be successful – let's start with the simple things. I think you have to be someone who is in touch with what is happening more widely than your organization. That is, in touch with other people, other networks and reading papers with an eye to what's coming, what's impacting. I think you have to be able to build very good relationships with a wide variety of people, from patients, right up to the dean of the medical school and the local MPs. You have to be someone who is prepared to work at relationships and build them. I think you must certainly be able to understand the finances of your organization and to look at what they signify. Although all my fellow chairs would not agree with this, I feel that you have to have an eye for the development of the organization, organizational behaviour and organizational structure. So, some organizational development issues, not in a professional sense but in terms of understanding what makes the organization tick.

You have to be able to look beyond the symptoms of what is happening and decide what might really be happening here, so that you can know what questions to ask to get to the root of it. I think you have to be personally authoritative and be comfortable with your own authority, but exercise it in a way that is engaging and warm, and respectful of other people. By comfortable, I mean that you have to be strong enough with your own sense of authority, that you are prepared to stand back and listen and not throw your weight around. People who have real personal authority find ways of exercising it that is enabling of others and I think that is absolutely key. You have to be organized, have a great sense of stewardship and probity and know what that means in reality.

In the health service in particular, you have to be prepared to tread this line between being the support and ambassador and steward of your own organization, and being prepared to see that your role is on behalf of the wider NHS. Where the needs of patients and the development of services conflict with your own organization, you don't get in a bunker – you get your organization out of that bunker. I host meetings of the chairs of all the trusts in our area and have a good working relationship with them, and I have said to them that we are responsible for the local NHS, not just for our own organizations. So where there have to be mergers and where we have to change services and be critical of our organizations, we are prepared to do that because of the greater good. You have to have people in the role who understand how to tread that line.

RAISING STANDARDS OF BOARD EFFECTIVENESS

Unless a board has completely abdicated its responsibility, its performance must have a significant impact on the performance of the company, particularly over the longer term. Improving the effectiveness of the board and raising its game is therefore vitally important to help in ensuring the ongoing prosperity and maybe survival of the organization itself. If the board is not as effective as it needs to be in today's fast changing and demanding environment, the company could well lose its way. In such circumstances the company may be acquired or bought out, involving changes to the board in either case. Alternatively, the shareholders may insist on board changes being made. The ultimate catastrophe would be for the company to founder completely.

Does your board regularly take a rigorous and objective look at itself and its pertinence to the ongoing needs of the company? Clearly, ignoring the issue of board effectiveness and its ongoing improvement is not an option. However good your board thinks it is, it can and must improve its effectiveness and adapt to meet the challenges of the future.

A comprehensive appraisal

The comprehensive approach to improving board performance starts with a fundamental review of the board, what it does and how. This must be done from a strategic perspective, against the changing background and likely needs of the company. The review will explore:

- the composition of the board;
- the matters it addresses;
- its style and processes;
- its focus.

When carrying out such a review, you may find it useful to refer to many of the issues explored and questions raised in this book, namely:

- *The composition of the board* – personal characteristics needed; achieving balance; board size and structure (see Chapter 5).
- *The matters it addresses* – directing, not managing; deciding major issues and delegating the rest (see Chapter 1). The key

'conditioning' and 'enterprise' tasks of the board (see Chapters 1, 2, 3 and 4).

- *Its style and processes* – planning and managing board meetings; boardroom behaviour; using board committees (see Chapter 6). Credibility, personalities, power and politics; using the non-executive directors (see Chapter 7). Decision making (see Chapter 1).
- *Its focus* – focusing on strategic issues; anticipating the future; corporate culture and values; thinking and acting strategically (see Chapter 2). Considering risk, compliance and ethics (see Chapter 4).

The results of this review must then be assessed by the board and consideration given to various ideas and options for improvement and change. The best way forward can then be agreed and plans made, followed by implementation and further review. The chairman usually leads this whole process, but many boards will use an external expert facilitator to help in carrying it out. You will find this book to be a useful aid in the course of planning and implementation.

An active review

While the comprehensive approach described above has definite benefits, some people favour a more pragmatic method of board appraisal. This process is usually quicker but less thorough than a comprehensive appraisal. Essentially, it poses a series of relevant questions for the board to address. The answers will help to highlight areas where board effectiveness is less than satisfactory. Where it is agreed that improvements are needed, the necessary action and timescales are determined and responsibilities allocated. Progress is then reported and a further review carried out to help ascertain what improvements have taken place and to see what new priorities there may be for improvement.

The whole procedure is usually led by the chairman and is carried out by the directors themselves, both individually and as a group. Each director is given a set of questions about the board and is asked to assess the board's effectiveness in each case by giving a mark out of 10. This must be done without colluding with other directors. Copies are then given to the chairman, who will examine them for points of consensus and have the responses consolidated.

The directors then meet to examine and discuss the results, agreeing and prioritizing which areas need improving and what action shall be taken, by whom and by when.

When this part is being undertaken, it is important to consider likely future needs as well as past performance. Often there will be a matter for the whole board to address and sometimes an individual or small group will be identified. Individuals can let the chairman know as progress is made and the board can then repeat the entire process in, say, six months, to review progress and agree new priorities.

If you intend to lead your board to undertake an active review of this nature, you may find the following lists of questions useful ones to employ. They can be used as they are, or modified to suit the particular circumstances of your board and organization.

How effective are our board meetings?

- Are objectives being achieved?
- Are we a well-informed board?
- Is the quality and depth of discussion good enough?
- Were our important decisions good?
- Do we seek the best advice when we need it?
- Are all the board's tasks being tackled effectively?
- Are only proper board issues being addressed?
- Are we an effective working group?
- Is everyone contributing and behaving effectively?
- Is the company's future prosperity being assured?

How well is our board doing in each of these areas?

- Determining the company's values and aspirations.
- Setting corporate vision / aims / mission / objectives.
- Contributing to strategic thinking and agreeing strategic plans.
- Ensuring availability of required resources.
- Ensuring reputation and achievements are protected.
- Determining and reviewing policies.
- Monitoring performance against plans, budgets and agreements.

- Monitoring adherence to laws, regulations and policies.
- Exercising responsibility to shareholders and other parties.

ASSESSING DIRECTORS' PERFORMANCE

Setting the criteria

An important factor in improving the effectiveness of your board, and therefore the success and prosperity of your organization, is for each individual director to become more competent as a board member. This has to be an ongoing process. It essentially requires that all directors clearly understand what is expected of them and what they must do to play their full part in elevating the board's performance. If yours is a typical board, this situation is unlikely to pertain.

The executive directors on your board will almost certainly have written job specifications that list the matters for which they are held responsible. Additionally, there may be specific objectives agreed annually that each director will be expected to achieve and against which his or her success will be judged. But do these job specifications and personal objectives relate solely to their executive management functions? If so, don't be surprised that the executive directors focus most of their energies and time on succeeding as executives and see their director roles as subsidiary extras to their perceived main purpose. Indeed, some may consider their director role largely as a status symbol. The fact is that while they are very clear about what is expected of them as executive managers, they are unlikely to have such a clear understanding of their role as board members and what they must do in that role to be successful *as directors.* This state of affairs is likely to be exacerbated if you are both chairman and chief executive/MD.

If there are non-executive directors on your board, can you be certain that they each know how well they are performing and what else they should do to improve their effectiveness? Do you give them feedback? Do they have a clear idea of what other directors think of their behaviour and the value that they add to the board's endeavours? Are regular reviews of such matters undertaken?

You may be using an *ad hoc* or informal approach to address these issues, but are you satisfied with the outcome? If you feel that improvements could be made, you might wish to consider more formal methods that are essentially simple, but effective. They follow practices that are regarded as customary in a management context but are, as yet, less than commonplace when dealing with directors. However, an increasing number of boards are using them.

The first step is to make clear to each director what specific responsibilities they have as members of your board, that is, *as directors.* You should undertake to discuss and agree a list of these responsibilities with each of the executive directors. It can then be included as a written statement forming part of their overall job specification, or kept as a separate document. It will also be useful for each of the non-executive directors to have such a written statement of their agreed responsibilities.

These responsibilities will span the matters that affect the way in which a director can add value to the board's deliberations, discussions, decision making and effectiveness. They will embrace matters of calibre and substance as well as process, and consider the distinct roles that each director may play. In the case of executive directors, these responsibilities are quite separate and distinct from any that they will have as a consequence of their management functions.

Assessing performance

A straightforward way of evaluating the performance of a director is to consider how well each of the agreed responsibilities has been carried out over, say, the past year. This process will help to identify areas for improvement in future, which can often be focused on specific actions. For example, it may be agreed that the marketing director should work on being better informed generally, with a specific requirement to become more financially aware. These agreed action points for improvement would then form a set of personal objectives for the director concerned.

A set of objectives formed in this way can be augmented by others that might be suggested by you. Essentially, these will be based on looking ahead rather than by reviewing the past. They can reflect how individuals could help in bringing about changes and improvements that you want to see achieved in the board's ways of working, style, focus and overall performance. This anticipatory method can help to reinforce any particular types of contribution and strength that each director would be expected to bring to the board to provide the overall balance and range of attributes, skills and knowledge required. It is a fundamentally positive approach, with none of the connotations of censure that some might feel when considering past imperfections.

Who should evaluate the directors and how? Although it can be argued that directors should be capable of self-appraisal, it is unlikely that we can really see ourselves as others do. One method that is often very effective is for the chairman to carry out a one-to-one appraisal of each director annually. In the case of executive directors, it is sensible to do this at a different time from any appraisals that take place relating to their executive management responsibilities. This helps to reinforce and separate their dual roles of director and manager.

An increasing number of boards have adopted a form of peer review in evaluating director performance that is often in addition to an appraisal by the chairman. One approach uses a universal list of areas of directors' responsibility that is drawn up as a result of a discussion on the subject by the whole board, under the chairman's guidance. Every director has a copy of the list for each colleague, on which an evaluation is made against each of the criteria, with brief supporting comments. They can be sent to the recipients anonymously or with the identity of the evaluator revealed, whichever is agreed beforehand. Security, discretion, respect and trust must all be evidenced for this process to be effective. Usually, that is the end of the peer review, which is not discussed between the participants – it is up to each individual to act upon the views expressed as they see fit. However, the issues raised may be brought up by the director during his or her subsequent one-to-one appraisal with the chairman and taken into account.

How should the performance of the chairman be appraised? There are several methods being used and you must judge which might be most appropriate in your situation. If the idea of being appraised is new to you, a cautious approach might be favoured, followed by something bolder later. On the other hand, if your board takes to the idea of a peer review right away, you may well feel obliged to join in the same process too. A range of options is shown below (in any case the list of chairman's attributes given earlier in this chapter could be used):

- candid feedback from the chief executive/MD, done in a structured way;
- review by the deputy chairman or a senior non-executive director whose views you respect;
- review by non-executive directors, either singly or together;
- using an independent consultant to make observations, take soundings and give feedback;
- individual peer review by the whole board.

Because the chief executive/MD has a unique and special role, there are aspects of his or her appraisal that should be carried out in a particular way. Since the chief executive/MD is charged with carrying through the decisions of the board, leading the organization's employees and managing the company day to day, a review of performance of such matters is called for. These embrace issues of company performance in relation to agreed plans and external benchmarks, as well as measures of the underlying health of the company.

Such a review is often best carried out formally by the chairman, with or without the support of one or more non-executive directors. Where the chairman is also the chief executive/MD, a senior non-executive director should be the appraiser. The appraisal can be structured around the areas of responsibility specified in the job description and list of powers delegated by the board. Any explicit personal objectives that were agreed previously should also be included. At the same time, a full review of the chief executive's performance as a member of the board team should be undertaken, as with the other directors. Obviously, the chief executive/MD would also normally be included in a peer review of contribution to board effectiveness by the whole board.

The Higgs report includes a section on performance evaluation guidance with lists of questions relating to boards of directors, the chairman and non-executive directors. The text is reproduced in Appendix 2 on pages 209–12.

An experienced chairman expressed the following views on some of the topics covered in this section

Linda Smith

The trick for a chair is to make the board function as a board that can really question whether we are making the progress we should. To do this, we must make sure that the executive directors can somehow don a different hat, even though in effect they are implicated in any criticisms we might make. It isn't easy, but then that's an issue for many boards in the private sector as well.

I have always had good vice-chairs, who can play a very important role in keeping me on track. I use my vice-chair to talk to about my own performance and to say, 'I am not sure I handled that well', 'I'm not sure that felt right', 'I'm not sure we are getting the best out of the board at the moment', and asking them what they think I should be doing differently. Sometimes I have asked them to be a process observer, to give me feedback afterwards when I feel that I am not handling things quite right. I feel comfortable having those checks on me. I also have a mentor, which I do think is quite important, both because I need to be challenged and to think and prepare for my role.

When I was first appointed, it took me a while to sort out what the things were that I was not very happy with. After about three or four months I was ready to do an initial appraisal – sitting down with the chief executive and asking how he thought he was doing and what he thought his objectives were and how the previous chair had appraised him. Then we explored what sort of systems we should have to do this and set it up. So it was after the first six months that we went into a formal appraisal. It took us the first year to get things right and there were ups and downs.

The chief executive and I sit down with each of the executive directors once a year to carry out an appraisal together. I have considered seeing them on my own but have decided against that. Since we reorganized and introduced this interview process, each of them has a job description that defines their roles as a director and as an executive separately. But we have an ongoing process too, where I talk to the executive directors quite frequently on an ad hoc basis, partly to keep them

> informed and also to hear about what they are doing. If I am unhappy about something which isn't being done, I will discuss it with the chief executive and we can think about how to raise it, and what to do about that. At the moment, six months on from the reorganization, we decided that we should have a review together, just to say how are you shaping up against these issues and the role, as set out in the job description.

DEVELOPING INDIVIDUAL DIRECTORS AND THE BOARD

Developing individual directors

Whatever appraisal procedure you and your board adopt, it will identify areas where individual directors could and should improve their effectiveness. One of your roles as chairman in this process is to give advice and guidance on what development methods would be appropriate. Such techniques could include the provision of some regular personal mentoring by you, perhaps in support of other ways of learning.

Remember that directors need to develop themselves and update their knowledge continuously to attain the levels of competence demanded by modern conditions. In doing so, they should be familiar with the wide range of learning methods and sources of information that are available to them, which include:

- distance learning, video and audio recordings;
- open and in-house courses, seminars and workshops;
- conferences;
- individual and group counselling;
- personal coaching and mentoring;
- information and opinion from colleagues and acquaintances;
- working on other boards as a non-executive director;
- on-the-job experience;
- books, journals and newspapers.

All directors must be familiar with their duties and responsibilities and the board's role in respect of the company and the many groups with an interest in it. In addition, every director should understand his or her specific role and function as part of the board and be familiar with the roles and functions of the other directors, in particular those of the chairman and chief executive/MD. Familiarity with a company balance sheet and profit and loss account, sources and methods of funding, cash flow and other financial parameters is essential for every director.

Any director who is uncertain of any of these matters should put the time aside for some structured learning, often in the form of a series of courses or workshops and/or reading or other learning media. This is, of course, a prerequisite for any person who is being appointed a director for the first time. Where the appointment is as a result of promotion, a proper course of study should ideally be undertaken before the appointment is made. In addition to these basic requirements, directors need to develop certain personal skills, acquire knowledge appropriate to their role and be constantly aware of the changing environment in which they and the company operate.

To maintain their effectiveness, non-executive directors should seek continually to develop and refresh their knowledge and skills to ensure that their contribution to the board remains informed and relevant. When asked to become a member of a board committee, they may well require specific training and familiarization with good practice and any regulatory requirements pertaining to the work of the committee.

Executive directors need to raise their awareness of governance matters and develop appropriate attitudes, knowledge and skills. This development includes loosening the power and rights that he or she is seen to have as a manager, or as a result of any exclusive technical knowledge held. This requires delegating more management authority, while raising his or her perceived strength as a director, concerned with policy, strategy, the company's reputation and security, and resource provision, and spending more time on such matters.

Each executive director should be encouraged to gain a degree of familiarity with the special contribution that each of the other executive directors can make, because of their particular experience, background and specialist knowledge. As part of this process, a sales director, for example, should spend time with the financial director to become familiar with the sum of his or her responsibilities and how his or her function operates. Some appropriate reading and attendance at selected courses or seminars can help to bring depth to such understanding.

This is a broadening process for each executive director, moving them away from the narrower confines of specialist management. At the same time, this process helps to weld the board into an effective team to address the wider policy and strategic issues. The benefit will be a really dynamic board where the full weight of collective experience, intellect, wisdom, knowledge, inspiration, creativity and pragmatism come to bear on the company's affairs to shape its future.

Development of the whole board

There are boards whose directors work so closely together in the day-to-day management of the business that they find it difficult to stand back collectively and concern themselves with policy and longer-term strategic matters. The situation applies particularly to the smaller company, whose directors often have a significant shareholding. The chairman of such a board may well benefit from advice and guidance from a suitably qualified consultant, who can help with the restructuring of board meetings and agenda items. Such guidance can also be used to school the whole board in changing its pattern of behaviour at board meetings.

The appointment of one or more non-executive directors onto such a board can be a great help in achieving the desired change of emphasis. Well-experienced, independent and knowledgeable non-executive directors will help to focus attention on the essential board issues by their insistence on addressing such matters. Their calibre and the breadth and weight of their experience and intellect can do wonders in developing an upper-grade management team into a really effective board.

Just as small company boards often have problems, so too do those of larger companies. In this case, the problem is often that there is not a proper team spirit. This can be because the non-executive directors, and also the chairman, do not know each other and the executive directors well enough as people, nor do they sufficiently understand the strength of each other's experience and background. One effective way to increase interpersonal knowledge among directors and to weld a better team is for all the directors to spend time together away from the work environment. This affords opportunities for social as well as business interchange and is often organized around the development of a new strategy, mission statement or reappraisal of the company's goals.

An effective way of developing the cohesiveness of the whole board is by using a sensitive, experienced consultant as counsellor. He or she will sit in on board meetings and then act as a constructive critic to the board while also giving counsel and guidance to each individual director, as necessary, rather like a tutor.

In these circumstances, time spent with the chairman can be most useful. Help can be given in seeing his or her own shortcomings, pointing the way to the development of new skills to improve personal performance. It can also help in understanding the reasons for clashes between directors, why difficult attitudes are often taken by individual directors and how better to overcome these problems. Improvements in these areas are made easier because the consultant will also be working with each director on a personal level, so that such problems can be tackled from both sides at once.

The processes of peer review of directors' personal performance as board members and the board effectiveness assessment techniques, described earlier in this chapter, can undoubtedly help greatly in developing the board. The positive feedback and both collective and individual commitment they produce are all major contributors to improving board effectiveness.

An experienced chairman expressed the following views on some of the topics covered in this section

Linda Smith

My own feeling is that there isn't an end point – that you never get to a position when you can say, 'Well, we've got this right'. This tension is something that has to be constantly managed and questioned and transparently dealt with. Everybody has to know that it is a tension and we work at it. Every so often we will review how we are doing as a board, question ourselves and think about our developing role and how we are managing that. There is a time when the board has to look at itself.

CHAPTER CHECKLIST

Here are some questions you might ask yourself in connection with the matters covered in this chapter before you plan any consequent action:

- Have you rated yourself against the list of attributes of the successful chairman listed on pages 172 and 173?
- ... or asked one or more of your fellow directors, or an observer, to assess your ability against them?
- ... and have you decided to undertake some personal development as a result of doing so?
- Does your board regularly take a rigorous and objective look at itself and its pertinence to the ongoing needs of the organization?
- Will your board undertake a comprehensive appraisal of its performance, exploring the board's composition, the matters it addresses, its style and processes, and its focus?
- ... or will you instead engage the board in an active review, using the lists of questions provided on pages 177–78?
- ... and in either case, will you ensure that improvement and change occur as a result?
- ... perhaps with the help of an experienced external consultant?
- Are you going to ensure that all the directors have a written list of their responsibilities as members of your board, spanning the matters that affect the way in which they can add value to the board's work?
- ... and will you be helping to evaluate their performance annually against these criteria and others suggested by you?
- Will you be evaluating the performance of the chief executive/MD against a broad range of criteria agreed with him or her, including performance as a member of the board team?
- Will you give guidance, advice and support to directors in connection with their personal development needs, including broadening the knowledge and attitudes of executive directors?
- ... ensuring that they at least fully understand their duties and responsibilities, the board's role and those of the other directors, and fundamental financial matters?

Appendix 1

Legal duties, liabilities and good practice

This summary, which is from *Standards for the Board* (The Institute of Directors, London, 2001), is for guidance only and refers to the duties and liabilities of company directors. *Standards for the Board* is currently being revised, so the content here reflects the law of England and Wales as at 1 March 2001 relating to directors of a company incorporated under the Companies Act 1985 (the 'Act'), various provisions of the Company Director's Disqualification Act 1986 and the Insolvency Act 1986, and also what is good practice in corporate governance. The Companies Acts apply to both Scotland and Wales. Matters of company law in Scotland are reserved to the UK Parliament under the Scotland Act 1998, and company law matters were not transferred to the Welsh National Assembly under the Government of Wales Act 1998. Companies in Northern Ireland are regulated under Orders that fully reflect the Companies Acts. The contents of this appendix are therefore applicable throughout the United Kingdom, save for a very few matters that are particular to Scotland.

The Company Law Reform Bill is expected to pass into law in 2007 and will change the law affecting companies, directors and other parties in several ways. The proposed changes have four themes:

1. enhancing shareholder engagement and a long-term investment culture;
2. ensuring better regulation and a 'Think Small First' approach;
3. making it easier to set up and run a company; and
4. providing flexibility for the future.

The DTI website provides further information.

Company directors should seek advice from their legal advisers if they are unclear about their current or potential legal position.

Guidance about the legal duties and liabilities of directors, together with useful references, is provided in *The Company Director's Guide* (IoD, 2001) and *The Director's Handbook* (IoD, 2005).

General

- A director is a person empowered under a company's Articles of Association to direct, and to share responsibility with the other directors for, the governance of its affairs. Directors are appointed in accordance with the Articles of the company, but it is possible, in law, for a person who has not been appointed or has been appointed improperly to assume the role of director (a 'shadow' director) and in so doing to become subject to many of the legal duties and obligations which apply to any director. This can also happen when a person engaged as an adviser is admitted to the decision making process of a board. While a person is not deemed a shadow director by reason only that the directors act on advice given by him or her in a professional capacity, if an adviser participates in making board decisions he or she may be deemed to be acting as a shadow director, and will be liable under some of the legal duties and obligations which apply to any director. For this reason, the formal status of people attending board meetings should be made clear by the chairman, when those other than board members are present.
- There is no single comprehensive legal code of conduct for directors. Their duties and liabilities arise under common law, the Act, and a variety of other statutes, regulations and rules.
- Directors' duties are owed to the company only. In addition, directors must have regard to the interests of the company's

shareholders, employees, the general public under certain environmental, health and safety legislation, and (if the company is or may be insolvent) creditors.

- All directors on the board share their legal responsibilities equally, whether they are executive or non-executive directors, and regardless of any particular duties under service agreements as employees.
- In general, directors are not liable for the company's debts or losses, unless they have given personal guarantees; but they may be made personally liable if they have acted in breach of their duties.
- For the purposes of wrongful trading, a director is judged by a legally defined standard. Failure to meet the standard may result in personal liability.

Constitutional powers

- Directors must not exceed the objects of the company under its Memorandum of Association, and must also operate within any limitations on their powers that may be imposed by its Articles.

Care and skill

- Directors must carry out their functions with reasonable skill, care and diligence and may be liable if they are negligent. A higher standard of care is required of a director who has particular skills or professional qualifications in relation to matters where those skills or qualifications have particular relevance.
- Directors should try to attend all board meetings, being absent only with good reason. Persistent non-attendance may amount to a breach of duty. Under the Articles of some companies the director may lose office if no board meetings are attended during a stated period.

Probity

Directors owe fiduciary duties to the company, which means that they are required to act in good faith in the best interests of the company; exercise their powers for the proper purposes for which they were conferred, and not place themselves in a position where there is a conflict (actual or potential) between their duties to the company and their personal interests (or the interests of any associated organization or person) or duties to third parties. Fiduciary obligations can apply in circumstances which are not always obvious, and where no intentional dishonesty is involved.

The implications of this arise in various ways. For example:

1. Boards should comply with relevant laws, regulations and codes or practice, refrain from anti-competitive practices, and honour obligations and commitments. Individual directors must at all times comply with the law and should endeavour to ensure that their company at all times complies with the law governing its operations.

2. Although not a legal obligation, each director should at all times respect the truth and act honestly in business dealings and in the exercise of all responsibilities as a director. It follows, for example, that a director should not obtain, attempt to obtain, or accept, any bribe, secret commission or illegal inducement of any sort. Integrity should be the hallmark of each board member's conduct in decision making, uninfluenced by shareholdings, or by business, political or personal commitments and relationships external to his or her company duties.

3. The company's assets and resources must be applied only for proper purposes. The directors will be liable for the loss caused to the company and/or to restore the company's assets if they misapply them.

4. The directors must exercise their powers and apply company assets and resources in the interests of the company, not for any ulterior purpose or to benefit themselves or anyone else.

5. As a rule, a director cannot enter into an agreement with a third party under which he or she fetters his or her power to exercise an independent judgement except where he or she believes in good faith that it is in the interest of the company to do so.

6. A director must not take advantage of his or her position as a director to gain, directly or indirectly, a personal advantage or an advantage for any associated person unless permitted by the company's constitution or the situation has been disclosed to the company in general meeting and the company has consented.

a. *A director must not make improper use of information acquired by virtue of his or her position as a director. This prohibition applies irrespective of whether or not the director or any associated person would gain directly or indirectly a personal advantage or whether or not the company might be harmed.*
b. *Directors should not use inside information for gain and will be liable to account to the company for their gain (ie profit not authorized by a shareholder resolution or in accordance with the company's Articles) if they use their position to make a secret profit.*
c. *A director should make sure that any information which is not in the public domain and which would have a significant effect on the company's share price if publicly available is not provided to anyone who may be influenced to subscribe for, buy or sell shares, or may advise others to do so. Such information includes, but is not limited to: profit forecasts, proposed share issues, borrowings, impending take-overs, impending litigation, significant changes in operations, new products, new discoveries, and financial problems. Listing Rules require directors of a company listed on the Stock Exchange to make adequate and timely disclosure to the Stock Exchange.*
d. *A director must not buy or sell shares while in possession of confidential information as a director of a company which, if disclosed publicly, would be likely materially to affect the price of the company's shares. It is good practice for the board to lay down precisely when shares can be traded by a director of the company, subject to legal or regulatory restrictions. Companies listed on the Stock Exchange must require their directors to comply with a code of dealing which is no less exacting than the Model Code of the Stock Exchange.*
e. *Good practice requires the board to develop guidelines on the circumstances in which benefits to be received by a director or an associated person are of sufficient magnitude that the approval of the shareholders should be sought, even if not required by law. The board should inform shareholders of these guidelines. A director of a company listed on the Stock Exchange must observe those Listing Rules relating to any benefits that a director or an associated person may receive from the company by way of an issue of shares or any other transaction of a similar nature.*

7. A company director has a general duty to avoid any actual or potential conflict between his or her own personal interests, or the interests of any associated organization or person, and his or her duties to the company.

   Under the Act, if a director, a member of his/her immediate family or other connected person (as defined by the Act) has a personal interest in some transaction involving the company, the director must declare that interest to the board.

   Directors must disclose to the company their interests (including the interests of their spouse and dependent children and certain trusts or companies controlled by such persons) in shares or debentures of the company (and group companies). The company is required to maintain a register, open to inspection, of these interests.

   Depending on the company's Articles, the director may be excluded from participating in a decision about or voting on a particular matter and/or from being counted in the quorum for the board meeting at which it is considered.

   In the extreme case of continuing material conflict of interest, good practice requires the director to resign from the board.

   Some examples where disclosure of interest would be appropriate are:

   a. *when a firm bids for a contract with the company, and a board member, or an associated party, has a financial interest in the firm or is a director of it;*
   b. *when a relative of a board member is on the staff or the board of an important supplier or customer;*
   c. *when a board member is party to information which is of commercial value to his or her own, or an associated party's, business or organization;*
   d. *when a director is appointed to a board at the instigation of a third party with a substantial interest in the company, such as a major shareholder or a creditor. The director's duty is to make a contribution in the interests of the company and not in the particular interest of the sponsor. If obligations to a third party preclude a director from taking an independent position on an issue, it is good practice to disclose the situation to the rest of the company board and it is for the board to judge whether or not the*

individual director should take part in the board's consideration of the particular issue.

In the examples above, or similar circumstances, confidential matters should not be disclosed to the interested parties without the prior agreement of the company board.

8. In general terms, members of a board should accept collective responsibility for the decisions of the board as loyal members of the board. This does not mean that a director should not be prepared, if necessary, to express disagreement with colleagues, including the chairman or managing director, but it does mean that he or she should accept that resignation or dismissal may sometimes be the ultimate consequence of sustained protest on a matter of company policy, conscience or principle.

   When a director concludes that he or she is unable to acquiesce in a decision of the board, some or all of the following steps should be considered:

   a. *making his/her dissent and its possible consequences clear to the board as a means of seeking to influence the decision;*
   b. *asking for additional legal, accounting or other professional advice (the* Combined Code *recommends that the company should meet the expenses incurred);*
   c. *asking that the decision be postponed to the next meeting to allow time for further consideration and informal discussion;*
   d. *tabling a statement of dissent or writing to the chairman and asking that the statement or letter be minuted;*
   e. *calling a special board meeting to consider the matter;*
   f. *resigning and considering advising the appropriate regulator.*

   A director who chooses to resign on a point of principle or other important matter should disclose the reasons for resignation to shareholders or to the appropriate regulator, though a director should bear in mind the duty not to disclose confidential information.

Transactions within the company

The Act imposes detailed restrictions on certain types of transaction between a company and any of its directors, their families, or other connected persons (as defined in the Act):

- Loans by a company to a director of more than £5,000 are prohibited, subject to certain detailed exceptions. Nor is the company allowed to provide a guarantee or other security for any loans to a director from another source. Any transaction entered into in contravention of these restrictions is voidable at the instance of the company and any director who authorizes the transaction is liable to account to the company for any gain that he or she has made by the transaction and to indemnify the company for any loss or damage resulting from the transaction. A director who authorized a company to enter into a transaction knowing or having reasonable cause to believe that the company was contravening these provisions is guilty of a criminal offence.
- Complex provisions of the Act deal with other types of credit transaction, which may be permitted in certain circumstances.
- A transfer of non-cash assets between a director, his family or other connected persons (as defined in the Act) and the company, where the value exceeds specified limits, is only permitted with the approval by resolution of the shareholders in general meeting, subject to detailed exceptions. If shareholder approval is not given, the transaction is voidable at the instance of the company and any director who authorized the transaction is liable to account to the company for any gain that he/she has made by the transaction and to indemnify the company for any loss or damage resulting from the transaction.
- Directors' service agreements under which the directors' employment may continue for a period of more than five years (during which period it cannot be terminated by the company by notice or can only be so terminated in specified circumstances) must be approved by resolution of the shareholders in general meeting. It is recommended here that service agreements are terminable on one year's notice.

Administration

- Directors are responsible for the company's due administration, including maintenance of proper accounting records, minutes of meetings, and filing information at Companies House. In practice the directors can delegate these duties and the company secretary may handle much of the administration, but this does not relieve the directors of the ultimate responsibility.

- There are numerous statutory provisions covering such topics as employee relations, health and safety, consumer protection, environmental protection, data protection and taxation. Some of these create offences of personal liability under which directors may face penalties if the company fails to comply with the statutory requirements.
- Directors are also subject to specific duties and restrictions under the Financial Services Act 2000, particularly in relation to the company's shares, in the case of a company limited by shares, and debentures.

Preparation of accounts

- Under the Act, the directors must ensure that proper accounting records are kept by the company, they must prepare and approve the annual report and accounts which comply with the Act, they must lay the accounts and report before the shareholders in general meeting and they must ensure that the company sends copies to all its shareholders and to the Registrar of Companies. The period allowed for laying and delivering the report and accounts is generally 10 months after the end of the relevant accounting reference period for a private company and seven months after the end of that period for a public company (with a three-month extension in each case for an overseas company).
- Small and medium-sized companies are exempt from certain requirements relating to the preparation of accounts. In addition, a private company may by resolution elect to dispense with the laying of accounts and report before the shareholders in general meeting. Such exemptions often apply in subsidiary companies.

Insolvency

If a company becomes or is about to become insolvent, the Insolvency Act 1986 imposes various duties and responsibilities on the directors, which are designed to protect the interests of the company's creditors. In particular:

- The directors may be liable for wrongful trading unless they took all proper steps to minimize the creditors' potential losses, once they knew or **ought to have concluded** that there was no reasonable prospect that insolvent liquidation could be avoided.

- Breach of this provision of the Insolvency Act 1986 may result in the directors being ordered by a court to contribute to the assets of the company, and / or disqualification.

Disqualification

- A director can be disqualified, under the Company Directors Disqualification Act 1986, from being a director or from otherwise being involved in the management of a company for any period between two and fifteen years in addition to incurring civil and criminal liabilities. A court must disqualify a director of a company which has at any time become insolvent where that person's conduct as a director makes him or her, in the court's opinion, unfit to be concerned in the 'management' (including direction) of a company. A court may also disqualify a director who has been guilty of serious or persistent offences in connection with the direction and / or management of a company, or who has been guilty of wrongful trading, fraud or breach of duty.
- A shareholder, as well as others, may apply to the court for a disqualification order. If a disqualified person acts as a director or is involved in the management of a company, he or she may be imprisoned for up to two years or fined or both and will be personally liable for the debts of that company.

Effectiveness

- The board should exercise leadership, enterprise and judgement, combined with prudent control, in directing the company so as to achieve its continuing prosperity, and always attempt to act in the best interests of the company as a whole. The board is responsible for ensuring that the company is financially viable and properly managed so as to protect and enhance the interests of the company over time. Each director should endeavour to ensure that the board fulfils its key purpose of safeguarding and improving the company's prosperity.
- The chairman of the board should endeavour to make certain that the role of the board and the key tasks of the board are properly understood by all the board members.
- Directors have a statutory duty of care and skill (see above).

Accountability

- The duties of the board are owed to the company, but, in evaluating the interests of the company, a board of directors is accountable to the shareholders as a whole for the stewardship of the company.
- In addition, various Acts of Parliament have imposed broader responsibilities on companies and directors so that directors must often evaluate their actions in a wide social context and must often be conscious of the impact of their business on society. Particular attention should be paid to the environment, questions of occupational health and safety, employee relations, equal opportunity for employees, the impact of competition rules and consumer protection rules, and other legislative and regulatory initiatives that may arise from time to time.
- Over and above any legal or regulatory constraints, in deciding what is in the best interest of the company and its continuing prosperity, the board may wish on occasion to take into account the interests of stakeholders where the board judges they have an appropriate interest in or influence over the achievement of company objectives and the way in which these objectives are achieved. In certain circumstances the board may judge that the company's intentions or actions should be explained or even justified to them. This is likely to be particularly the case at times of major change or crisis (for example, large redundancy programmes, environmental disasters, take-over bids).

Openness

- Although not a legal obligation, it is good practice for directors to be as open and honest with their boards as possible.
- The board is responsible for communicating fully with shareholders and aligning the company with the latters' interests. The board must ensure the company complies with its legal obligations as to the disclosure of information.
- There should be sufficient transparency about the activities of the board in particular, and the company in general, to secure the confidence and trust of employees, customers, suppliers and the community which the company serves, without sacrificing commercial confidentiality. Reasonable transparency is a

prerequisite for worthwhile relationships with all the parties associated with a company. This goes beyond the duty that directors owe to the company and beyond the discharge of their duties of disclosure created by the Act.

- However, the board must take care to protect such information as the company holds in confidence. This applies equally to commercially and personally confidential information affecting the company and its employees, customers, suppliers, business partners or others. In addition, the company must comply with the legislation on data protection.
- Similarly, a director must not disclose, or allow to be disclosed, confidential information received in the course of the exercise of his/her duties as a director, unless that disclosure has been authorized by the board of the company or is required by law. Trade secrets, matters that are an intellectual property right of the company, processes and methods, advertising and promotional programmes, and statistics affecting financial results, in particular, must not be disclosed.
- It is good practice for the board to ensure that there is a policy on openness and confidentiality of information which it regularly monitors and reviews. The board should also ensure that its own actions are consistent with this policy.

Director development

- Boards should try to ensure that all directors keep abreast of both practical and theoretical developments in company direction to ensure that their expertise is constantly relevant. Continuous and rapid change is the norm in business and it is the responsibility of a director continually and systematically to add to his or her knowledge, skill and expertise; it is not enough to match present good practice and thereafter regard oneself as adequately equipped for the future.

Appendix 2

Corporate governance issues and the *Combined Code on Corporate Governance*

The practice of good corporate governance should be of concern to all boards of directors. Although the topic is of particular relevance to directors of companies whose shares are traded publicly, it has also become a matter of increasing interest and pertinence to boards of other companies and corporate bodies in recent years – a trend that is set to continue. This is why competent chairmen should become familiar with the issues and trends in corporate governance and consider which aspects might be applicable to the boards of their organizations and when.

In this context, the broadening of the responsibilities undertaken by non-executive directors and the growing importance of their contribution to board balance and effectiveness are important developments. The review carried out by Derek Higgs on the role and effectiveness of non-executive directors and the Tyson report on their recruitment and development, both published in 2003, have been formative in this regard and are recommended reading for chairmen. Some highlights from these publications are reproduced below.

In the context of the chairman's responsibilities and concerns and matters examined in this book it is pertinent to reproduce extracts here from the *Code* text and the Higgs report for reference, on the following topics: The Board, non-executive director independence, Guidance for the Chairman and Non-executive Directors and Performance Evaluation Guidance, the last three pertaining to the Higgs report. There are also summaries of the matters contained in the Tyson report on recruitment and development of non-executive directors and the Smith report on guidance for audit committees.

As an aid to wider reading on corporate governance matters, a list of useful web links and books published in the last few years is included in this appendix.

THE COMBINED CODE

The boards of companies quoted on the London Stock Exchange must be aware of the requirements set out in the *Combined Code on Corporate Governance*. However, the document also forms a touchstone that other organizations can use in developing their own corporate governance models and practices. Copies are available from the Financial Reporting Council and can be viewed on their website (given below). The topics covered are grouped under the following headings:

- A Directors
- B Remuneration
- C Accountability and Audit
- D Relations with Shareholders
- E Institutional Shareholders

There are also schedules covering:

- Provisions on the design of performance related remuneration
- Guidance on liability of non-executive directors: care skill and diligence
- The disclosure of corporate governance arrangements

The following extract from the preamble in the *Code* document contains some interesting matters, particularly with regard to compliance:

> *This* Code *supersedes and replaces the* Combined Code *issued in 2003. It follows a review by the Financial Reporting Council of the implementation of the* Code *in 2005 and subsequent consultation on possible amendments to the* Code.
>
> *The Financial Services Authority, as the UK Listing Authority, is obliged by statute to carry out a separate consultation before listed companies can be formally required under the Listing Rules to disclose how they have applied this new version of the* Combined Code. *This consultation is expected to begin in September 2006 and, subject to views received, the Listing Rules would be expected to apply to the new version of the* Combined Code *with effect from some time in the second quarter of 2007.*
>
> *In the meantime, in view of the limited nature of the changes and the strong support that they have received, the FRC would encourage companies and investors to apply the revised* Code *voluntarily for reporting years beginning on or after 1 November 2006.*
>
> *The* Code *contains main and supporting principles and provisions. The existing Listing Rules require listed companies to make a disclosure statement in two parts in relation to the* Code. *In the first part of the statement, the company has to report on how it applies the principles in the* Code. *In future this will need to cover both main and supporting principles. The form and content of this part of the statement are not prescribed, the intention being that companies should have a free hand to explain their governance policies in the light of the principles, including any special circumstances applying to them which have led to a particular approach. In the second part of the statement the company has either to confirm that it complies with the* Code's *provisions or – where it does not – to provide an explanation. This 'comply or explain' approach has been in operation for over ten years and the flexibility it offers has been widely welcomed both by company boards and by investors. It is for shareholders and others to evaluate the company's statement.*
>
> *While it is expected that listed companies will comply with the* Code's *provisions most of the time, it is recognised that departure from the provisions of the* Code *may be justified in particular circumstances. Every company must review each provision carefully and give a considered explanation if it departs from the* Code *provisions.*
>
> *Smaller listed companies, in particular those new to listing, may judge that some of the provisions are disproportionate or less relevant in their case.*
>
> *Some of the provisions do not apply to companies below FTSE 350. Such companies may nonetheless consider that it would be appropriate to adopt the approach in the* Code *and they are encouraged to consider this.*

Investment companies typically have a different board structure, which may affect the relevance of particular provisions.

Whilst recognising that directors are appointed by shareholders who are the owners of companies, it is important that those concerned with the evaluation of governance should do so with common sense in order to promote partnership and trust, based on mutual understanding. They should pay due regard to companies' individual circumstances and bear in mind in particular the size and complexity of the company and the nature of the risks and challenges it faces. Whilst shareholders have every right to challenge companies' explanations if they are unconvincing, they should not be evaluated in a mechanistic way and departures from the Code *should not be automatically treated as breaches. Institutional shareholders and their agents should be careful to respond to the statements from companies in a manner that supports the 'comply or explain' principle. As the principles in Section 2 make clear, institutional shareholders should carefully consider explanations given for departure from the* Code *and make reasoned judgements in each case. They should put their views to the company and be prepared to enter a dialogue if they do not accept the company's position. Institutional shareholders should be prepared to put such views in writing where appropriate.*

Nothing in this Code *should be taken to override the general requirements of law to treat shareholders equally in access to information.*

The current version of the *Combined Code* was published in June 2006. Most listed companies reported against the 2003 *Combined Code* for the first time in 2005.

- amending section D.2 to provide shareholders voting by proxy with the option of withholding their vote, and to require the publication of details of proxies lodged at the AGM where votes are taken on a show of hands; and
- for those provisions that require companies to 'make information available' (provisions A.4.1, B.2.1 and C.3.3), enabling the requirement to be met by placing the information on the company's website.

The board

Main principle: every company should be headed by an effective board that is collectively responsible for the success of the company. **Supporting principles:** The board's role is to provide entrepreneurial leadership of the company within a framework of prudent and effective controls which enables risk to be assessed and managed. The board should set the company's strategic aims, ensure that the necessary financial and human resources are in place for the company to meet its objectives and review management performance. The board should set the company's values and standards and ensure that its obligations to its shareholders and others are understood and met.

All directors must take decisions objectively in the interests of the company.

As part of their role as members of a unitary board, non-executive directors should constructively challenge and help develop proposals on strategy. Non-executive directors should scrutinize the performance of management in meeting agreed goals and objectives and monitor the reporting of performance. They should satisfy themselves on the integrity of financial information and that financial controls and systems of risk management are robust and defensible. They are responsible for determining appropriate levels of remuneration of executive directors and have a prime role in appointing, and where necessary removing, executive directors, and in succession planning.

(The Code Provisions relating to this sub-section are then listed.)

Code provisions regarding non-executive director independence

The board should identify in the annual report each non-executive director it considers to be independent. The board should determine whether the director is independent in character and judgement and whether there are relationships or circumstances which are likely to affect, or could appear to affect, the director's judgement. The board should state its reasons if it determines that a director is independent notwithstanding the existence of relationships or circumstances which may appear relevant to its determination, including if the director:

- has been an employee of the company or group within the last five years;
- has, or has had within the last three years, a material business relationship with the company either directly, or as a partner, shareholder, director or senior employee of a body that has such a relationship with the company;

- has received or receives additional remuneration from the company apart from a director's fee, participates in the company's share option or a performance-related pay scheme, or is a member of the company's pension scheme;
- has close family ties with any of the company's advisers, directors or senior employees;
- holds cross-directorships or has significant links with other directors through involvement in other companies or bodies;
- represents a significant shareholder; or
- has served on the board for more than nine years from the date of their first election.

THE HIGGS REPORT

The report was published in 2003 as a review of the role and effectiveness of non-executive directors on the boards of listed companies. Many of the recommendations are now reflected in the Combined Code on Corporate Governance. They include the following topics: The board; the chairman; non-executive directors' role, independence, recruitment, appointment, induction, professional development, tenure, time commitment, remuneration, resignation and liability. Recommendations on audit and remuneration committees and relationships with shareholders are also covered.

The report includes useful annexes on the following topics:

a) Guidance for the chairman

b) Guidance for non-executive directors

c) Summary of the principal duties of the remuneration committee

d) Summary of the principal duties of the nomination committee

e) Pre-appointment due diligence checklist for new board members

f) Sample letter of non-executive director appointment

g) Induction checklist

h) Performance evaluation checklist

Guidance on the role of the chairman

The chairman is pivotal in creating the conditions for overall board and individual director effectiveness, both inside and outside the boardroom. Specifically, it is the responsibility of the chairman to:

- run the board and set its agenda. The agenda should take full account of the issues and the concerns of all board members. Agendas should be forward looking and concentrate on strategic matters rather than formulaic approvals of proposals which can be the subject of appropriate delegated powers to management;
- ensure that the members of the board receive accurate, timely and clear information, in particular about the company's performance, to enable the board to take sound decisions, monitor effectively and provide advice to promote the success of the company;
- ensure effective communication with shareholders and ensure that the members of the board develop an understanding of the views of the major investors;
- manage the board to ensure that sufficient time is allowed for discussion of complex or contentious issues, where appropriate arranging for informal meetings beforehand to enable thorough preparation for the board discussion. It is particularly important that non-executive directors have sufficient time to consider critical issues and are not faced with unrealistic deadlines for decision-making;
- take the lead in providing a properly constructed induction programme for new directors that is comprehensive, formal and tailored, facilitated by the company secretary;
- take the lead in identifying and meeting the development needs of individual directors, with the company secretary having a key role in facilitating provision. It is the responsibility of the chairman to address the development needs of the board as a whole with a view to enhancing its overall effectiveness as a team;
- ensure that the performance of individuals and of the board as a whole and its committees is evaluated at least once a year; and
- encourage active engagement by all the members of the board.

The effective chairman:

- upholds the highest standards of integrity and probity;
- sets the agenda, style and tone of board discussions to promote effective decision-making and constructive debate;
- promotes effective relationships and open communication, both inside and outside the boardroom, between non-executive directors and the executive team;
- builds an effective and complementary board, initiating change and planning succession in board appointments, subject to board and shareholders' approval;
- promotes the highest standards of corporate governance and seeks compliance with the provisions of the *Code* wherever possible;
- ensures clear structure for and the effective running of board committees;
- ensures effective implementation of board decisions;
- establishes a close relationship of trust with the chief executive, providing support and advice while respecting executive responsibility; and
- provides coherent leadership of the company, including representing the company and understanding the views of shareholders.

Guidance on the role of the non-executive director

As members of the unitary board, all directors are required to:

- provide entrepreneurial leadership of the company within a framework of prudent and effective controls that enable risk to be assessed and managed;
- set the company's strategic aims, ensure that the necessary financial and human resources are in place for the company to meet its objectives, and review management performance; and
- set the company's values and standards and ensure that its obligations to its shareholders and others are understood and met.

In addition to these requirements for all directors, the role of the non-executive director has the following key elements:

- **Strategy.** Non-executive directors should constructively challenge and help develop proposals on strategy.
- **Performance.** Non-executive directors should scrutinize the performance of management in meeting agreed goals and objectives and monitor the reporting of performance.
- **Risk.** Non-executive directors should satisfy themselves on the integrity of financial information and that financial controls and systems of risk management are robust and defensible.
- **People.** Non-executive directors are responsible for determining appropriate levels of remuneration of executive directors, and have a prime role in appointing, and where necessary removing, executive directors and in succession planning.

Non-executive directors should constantly seek to establish and maintain confidence in the conduct of the company. They should be independent in judgement and have an enquiring mind. To be effective, non-executive directors need to build a recognition by executives of their contribution in order to promote openness and trust.

To be effective, non-executive directors need to be well-informed about the company and the external environment in which it operates, with a strong command of issues relevant to the business. A non-executive director should insist on a comprehensive, formal and tailored induction. An effective induction need not be restricted to the boardroom, so consideration should be given to visiting sites and meeting senior and middle management. Once in post, an effective non-executive director should seek continually to develop and refresh their knowledge and skills to ensure that their contribution to the board remains informed and relevant.

Best practice dictates that an effective non-executive director will ensure that information is provided sufficiently in advance of meetings to enable thorough consideration of the issues facing the board. The non-executive should insist that information is sufficient, accurate, clear and timely.

An element of the role of the non-executive director is to understand the views of major investors both directly and through the chairman and the senior independent director.

The effective non-executive director:

- upholds the highest ethical standards of integrity and probity;
- supports executives in their leadership of the business while monitoring their conduct;
- questions intelligently, debates constructively, challenges rigorously and decides dispassionately;
- listens sensitively to the views of others, inside and outside the board;
- gains the trust and respect of other board members; and
- promotes the highest standards of corporate governance and seeks compliance with the provisions of the *Code* wherever possible.

Performance evaluation guidance

Guidance on performance evaluation

The *Code* provides that the board should undertake a formal and rigorous annual evaluation of its own performance and that of its committees and individual directors. Individual evaluation should aim to show whether each director continues to contribute effectively and to demonstrate commitment to the role (including commitment of time for board and committee meetings and any other duties). The chairman should act on the results of the performance evaluation by recognizing the strengths and addressing the weaknesses of the board and, where appropriate, proposing new members be appointed to the board or seeking the resignation of directors. The board should state in the annual report how such performance evaluation has been conducted.

It is the responsibility of the chairman to select an effective process and to act on its outcome. The use of an external third party to conduct the evaluation will bring objectivity to the process.

The non-executive directors, led by the senior independent director, should be responsible for performance evaluation of the chairman, taking into account the views of executive directors.

The evaluation process will be used constructively as a mechanism to improve board effectiveness, maximize strengths and tackle weaknesses. The results of board evaluation should be shared with the board as a whole while the results of individual assessments should remain confidential between the chairman and the non-executive director concerned.

The following are some of the questions that should be considered in a performance evaluation. They are, however, by no means definitive or exhaustive and companies will wish to tailor the questions to suit their own needs and circumstances.

The responses to these questions and others should enable boards to assess how they are performing and to identify how certain elements of their performance areas might be improved.

Performance evaluation of the board

- How well has the board performed against any performance objectives that have been set?
- What has been the board's contribution to the testing and development of strategy?
- What has been the board's contribution to ensuring robust and effective risk management?
- Is the composition of the board and its committees appropriate, with the right mix of knowledge and skills to maximize performance in the light of future strategy? Are inside and outside the board relationships working effectively?
- How has the board responded to any problems or crises that have emerged and could or should these have been foreseen?
- Are the matters specifically reserved for the board the right ones?
- How well does the board communicate with the management team, company employees and others? How effectively does it use mechanisms such as the AGM and the annual report?
- Is the board as a whole up-to-date with latest developments in the regulatory environment and the market?
- How effective are the board's committees? (Specific questions on the performance of each committee should be included such as, for example, their role, their composition and their interaction with the board.)

The processes that help underpin the board's effectiveness should also be evaluated eg:

- is appropriate, timely information of the right length and quality provided to the board and is management responsive to requests for clarification or amplification? Does the board provide helpful feedback to management on its requirements?
- Are sufficient board and committee meetings of appropriate length held to enable proper consideration of issues? Is time used effectively?
- Are board procedures conducive to effective performance and flexible enough to deal with all eventualities?

In addition, there are some specific issues relating to the chairman which should be included as part of an evaluation of the board's performance eg:

- Is the chairman demonstrating effective leadership of the board?
- Are relationships and communications with shareholders well managed?
- Are relationships and communications within the board constructive?
- Are the processes for setting the agenda working? Do they enable board members to raise issues and concerns?
- Is the company secretary being used appropriately and to maximum value?

Performance evaluation of the non-executive director

The chairman and other board members should consider the following issues and the individual concerned should also be asked to assess themselves. For each non-executive director:

- How well prepared and informed are they for board meetings and is their meeting attendance satisfactory?
- Do they demonstrate a willingness to devote time and effort to understand the company and its business and a readiness to participate in events outside the boardroom such as site visits?
- What has been the quality and value of their contributions at board meetings?

- What has been their contribution to development of strategy and to risk management?
- How successfully have they brought their knowledge and experience to bear in the consideration of strategy?
- How effectively have they probed to test information and assumptions? Where necessary, how resolute are they in maintaining their own views and resisting pressure from others?
- How effectively and proactively have they followed up their areas of concern?
- How effective and successful are their relationships with fellow board members, the company secretary and senior management? Does their performance and behaviour engender mutual trust and respect within the board?
- How actively and successfully do they refresh their knowledge and skills and are they up to date with:
  a. the latest developments in areas such as corporate governance framework and financial reporting?
  b. the industry and market conditions?
- How well do they communicate with fellow board members, senior management and others, for example shareholders? Are they able to present their views convincingly yet diplomatically and do they listen and take on board the views of others?

THE TYSON REPORT

Executive Summary

The report by Derek Higgs on the 'Role and Effectiveness of Non-executive Directors' raised the agenda of boardroom effectiveness. This report provides another piece of the jigsaw by highlighting how a range of different backgrounds and experiences among board members can enhance board effectiveness and by exploring how a broader range of non-executive directors can be identified and recruited.

The selection of each non-executive director (NED) should rest on a careful assessment of the needs and challenges of a particular company and on a broad, transparent and rigorous search that reflects this assessment.

Factors such as a company's size and age, the makeup of its customer and employee base, the extent of its participation in global markets, its future strategies, and its current board membership are important determinants of its NED requirements.

Diversity in the backgrounds, skills, and experiences of NEDs enhances board effectiveness by bringing a wider range of perspectives and knowledge to bear on issues of company performance, strategy and risk. Board diversity can also send a positive and motivating signal to customers, shareholders and employees, and can contribute to a better understanding by the company's leadership of the diverse constituencies that affect its success. Broader, more rigorous and more transparent search processes for NEDs would not only enhance board talent and effectiveness but would also foster greater diversity in the background, experience, age, gender, ethnicity and nationality of NED.

Many UK companies would benefit from extending their searches for NEDs to new pools of talent. Possible sources of talented candidates that traditional, largely informal, search processes have tended to overlook include: the so-called 'marzipan' layer of corporate management just below board level; unlisted companies and private equity firms; business services and consultancies; and organizations in the noncommercial sector.

In addition, despite the increasing globalization of business, the NEDs of UK companies tend to be domestic citizens rather than foreign nationals. Such board membership represents a potential mismatch between the international issues a company faces and the knowledge that its domestic board members can bring. Such a mismatch is likely to compromise the global competitive strength of British-based companies over time.

To help individuals from non-traditional sources who want to be considered for NED positions, we describe the role of executive search firms in identifying potential NED candidates and we suggest what individuals can do to be considered for these positions. We also note that a growing number of non-commercial organizations, such as the Association of Chief Executives of Voluntary Organizations (ACEVO), are developing databases of qualified individuals interested in NED positions.

Individuals with successful leadership careers in the non-commercial and public sectors have the attributes, skills and experience relevant to commercial NED positions. We provide information showing that large non-commercial organizations are comparable in scale and complexity to large commercial organizations.

We decided against developing our own list of qualified candidates of individuals from the non-commercial sector with the skills and experience relevant to NED positions in the commercial sector. Developing a list of candidates without a careful assessment of company needs and without a broad, rigorous and transparent search process would be inconsistent with our recommendations about how companies should select their NEDs.

As NED responsibilities continue to expand, companies will have to provide more training and evaluation for their board members. Companies should provide thorough induction programmes for all new NED appointees and should provide ongoing training opportunities for incumbent NEDs. Companies should also evaluate the performance of their boards on a regular basis, and NED training should be linked to the findings of such assessments. Training and evaluation processes are likely to be particularly important for companies committed to building diverse boards and to realizing the benefits of diversity among their members.

Although board training is currently available in a variety of ways, there are possible gaps between what providers of training are offering and what companies need. We recommend an initiative to bring together companies and training providers to establish guidelines to ensure that training programmes for directors are providing what is needed, and that useful information about such programmes is easily accessible on a timely basis. London Business School has offered to play a full part in such discussions.

We recommend an initiative to monitor both progress on achieving rigorous and transparent processes for NED appointments and progress on building more diverse boardrooms. Such an initiative should provide reliable measures of board composition for individual companies, should disseminate best-practice examples of how individual companies build more diverse and meritocratic boards, and should foster research on the impact of board diversity on board and company performance. Optimizing board membership is vital for company performance and competitiveness. It can also play an important role in restoring shareholder and public trust in UK boardrooms.

This guidance is closely based on Sir Robert Smith's proposed guidance published in January 2003. It deals comprehensively with all aspects of the audit committee and its relationships with other parties.

Specific topics covered include the establishment and role of the audit committee, its membership and appointment, procedures and resources, including the remuneration, skills, experience and training of committee members. There are sections on the relationship with the board and the role and responsibilities of the committee, including financial reporting, internal financial controls and risk management systems, whistleblowing and the internal and external audit processes. Communication with shareholders is also dealt with.

SOME PUBLICATIONS ON CORPORATE GOVERNANCE, 2000–2006

Banks E (2004) *Corporate Governance: Financial responsibility, controls and ethics,* Palgrave Macmillan, Basingstoke

Boleat M (2000) *Good Practice in Trade Association Governance,* Plaza, London

Bruce M (2004) *The ICSA Director's Guide,* ICSA Publishing, London

Bruce M (2005) *Rights and Duties of Directors,* Tottel's Publishing, Haywards Heath

Cadbury A (2002) *Corporate Governance and Chairmanship: A personal view,* Oxford University Press, Oxford

Carlsson R (2001) *Ownership and Value Creation: Strategic corporate governance in the new economy,* Wiley, Chichester

Carter C & Lorsch J (2004) *Back to the Drawing Board: Designing corporate boards for a complex world,* Harvard Business School Press, Boston

Carver J (2002) *On Board Leadership: Selected writings from the creator of the world's most provocative and systematic governance model,* Jossey-Bass, San Fransisco

Carver J & Oliver C (2002) *Corporate Boards that Create Value: Governing company performance from the boardroom,* Jossey-Bass, San Francisco

Chambers A (2005) *Tottel's Corporate Governance Handbook,* Tottel's Publishing, Haywards Heath

Charkham J, Global Corporate Governance Forum (2004) *Guidance for the Directors of Banks*, The World Bank, Washington

Charkham J (2005) *Keeping Better Company: Corporate governance ten years on*, Oxford University Press, Oxford

Chew D & Gillan S (2004) *Corporate Governance at the Crossroads: A book of readings*, McGraw-Hill Irwin, London

Colley J, Doyle J, Logan G & Stettinius W (2005) *Corporate Governance*, McGraw-Hill, London

Cooper B (2004) *The ICSA Handbook of Good Boardroom Practice*, ICSA Publishing, London

Cornforth C (ed) (2003) *The Governance of Public and Non-profit Organisations: What do boards do?*, Routledge, London

Corporate Governance: The Practical Guide for Directors 2nd Edition (2003) IR Publications, London

Corporate Governance in a Changing Economic and Political Environment: Trajectories of institutional change (2003) Palgrave Macmillan, Basingstoke

Coyle B (2004) *Risk Awareness and Corporate Governance*, Financial World, London

Coyle B (2005) *The ICSA Corporate Governance Handbook*, ICSA Publishing, London

Dallas G (2004) *Governance and Risk: An analytical handbook for investors, managers, directors and stakeholders*, McGraw Hill, New York

David F (2003) *Boards that Work: A guide for charity trustees*, Directory of Social Change, London

The Development of Corporate Governance in Britain and Japan (2004), Ashgate, Aldershot

Euromoney (2004) *International Corporate Governance Review 2004*, Euromoney, Colchester

Fahy M, Roche J & Weiner A (2005) *Beyond Governance: Creating corporate value through performance, conformance and responsibility*, John Wiley & Sons, Chichester

Financial Reporting Council (2003) *The Combined Code on Corporate Governance*, FRC, London

Fitzgerald P (2001) *Corporate Governance in the Public & Voluntary Sectors*, RSA, Bristol

Fraser I & Henry W (2003) *The Future of Corporate Governance: Insights from the UK*, Institute of Chartered Accountants of Scotland, Edinburgh

Fraser I & Henry W (2000) *The Future of Corporate Governance: Insights from the Netherlands,* Institute of Chartered Accountants in Scotland

Friedman A Phillips M & Chan Ming J D (2002) *Governance of Professional Organisations: The structure and role of the governing body,* PARN, Bristol

Garratt B (2003) *Thin on Top: Why corporate governance matters and how to measure and improve board performance,* Nicholas Brealey Publishing, London

Global Corporate Governance Forum (2004) *Building Director Training Organizations,* The World Bank, Washington

Hancock J (ed) (2004) *Investing in Corporate Social Responsibility: A guide to best practice, business planning and the UK's leading companies,* Kogan Page, London

Higgs D (2003) *Review of the Role and Effectiveness of Non-executive Directors,* DTI, London

Incomes Data Services (2005) *Corporate governance: IDS compliance guide,* Incomes Data Services, London

Institute of Directors (2004) *Corporate Governance: Practical advice for directors on today's most important boardroom issues,* IoD, London

Institute of Directors (2004) *The handbook of international corporate governance: a definitive guide,* Kogan Page, London

Institute of Directors (2005) *Corporate Governance: What should the government be doing?,* Institute of Directors, London

International Corporate Governance: Strategic action plans for management and investors, 2nd Edition (2004) Euromoney Books, London

IR Publications (2003) *Corporate governance: The practical guide for directors,* IR Publications, London

Iskander M R & C N *Corporate Governance: A framework for implementation,* World Bank, Washington DC

Keasey K, Thompson S & Wright M (2005) *Corporate Governance: Accountability, enterprise and international comparisons,* John Wiley & Sons, Chichester

Leipziger D (2003) *The Corporate Responsibility Codebook,* Greenleaf, Sheffield

MaCavoy P & Millstein I (2003) *The Recurrent Crisis in Corporate governance,* Palgrave Macmillan, Basingstoke

Mallin C (2004) *Corporate governanee,* Oxford University Press, Oxford

Merson R (2003) *Non-executive Directors: A BDO Stoy Hayward guide for growing businesses,* Profile Books, London

Monks R & Minow N (2004) *Corporate Governance*, 3rd Edition, Blackwell, Oxford

National Association of Pension Funds (2002) *Independent Directors – what investors expect*, NAPF, London

O'Brien J (2005) *Governing the corporation: Regulation and corporate governance in an age of scandal and global markets*, John Wiley & Sons, Chichester

O'Sullivan M (2000) *Contests for Corporate Control: Corporate governance and economic performance in the United States and Germany*, Oxford University Press, Oxford

Peter P (2003) *The Combined Code: An analysis of the main changes*, Institute of Directors, London

Roe M J (2003) *Political Determinants of Corporate Governance: Political context, corporate impact*, Oxford University Press, New York

Sheikh S (2003) *A Practical Approach to Corporate Governance*, Lexis Nexis, London

Smerdon R (2004) *A Practical Guide to Corporate Governance, 2nd Edition*, Sweet and Maxwell, London

Smithson J (2004) *The Role of the Non-executive Director in the Small to Medium-sized Business*, Palgrave Macmillan, Basingstoke

Solomon J & Solomon A (2004) *Corporate Governance and Accountability*, John Wiley & Sons, Chichester

Spencer S (2005) *Spencer Stuart Governance Lexicon: A director's guide to corporate governance around the world 2005/6*, Spencer Stuart, London

Sternberg E (2004) *Corporate Governance: Accountability in the marketplace*, Institute of Economic Affairs, London

Tickell J (2005) *Good governance: A code for the voluntary and community sector*, National Council for Voluntary Organisations, London

Warren R C (2000) *Corporate Governance and Accountability*, Liverpool, Academic Press, Bromborough

CORPORATE GOVERNANCE – USEFUL WEB LINKS

The Combined Code on Corporate Governance www.frc.org.uk/combinedcode.cfm

The Higgs Review (2003), together with full details of the research conducted for the Review and related information: http://www.dti.gov.uk/cld/non_exec_review

The Cadbury Report (1992), Greenbury Report (1995) and Hampel Report (1998): http://www.ecgi.org/codes/country_pages/codes_uk.htm

The Smith Report (2003): http://www.frc.org.uk/publications/content/ACReport.pdf http://www.ecgi.org/codes/country_documents/uk/ac_report.pdf

The Financial Services Authority's Listing Rules (2002) (see in particular paragraph 12.43A): http://www.fsa.gov.uk/pubs/ukla/

Corporate governance codes in other countries: http://www.ecgi.org/codes/all_codes.htm

Information on the Company Law Review (2001) and the Company Law White Paper (2002): http://www.dti.gov.uk/cld/

Copies of guidance produced by the Institute of Chartered Secretaries and Administrators: http://www.icsa.org.uk

The Institutional Shareholders' Committee's document 'The Responsibilities of Institutional Shareholders and Agents – Statement of Principles' (2002): http://www.investmentuk.org/press/2002/20021021-01.pdf

The Tyson report on the Recruitment and Development of Non-Executive Directors (2003): http://www.london.edu/tysonreport/Tyson_Report_June_2003.pdf

The Myners Report on Institutional Investment in the UK (2001): http://www.hm-treasury.gov.uk/media//843F0/31.pdf

The Directors' Remuneration Report Regulations 2002: http://www.hmso.gov.uk/si/si2002/20021986.htm

The DTI Consultation document '"Rewards for Failure": Directors' Remuneration – Contracts, Performance and Severance', (2003): http://www.dti.gov.uk/cld/4864rewards.pdf

The report of the EU High Level Group of Company Law Experts (the 'Winter group') (2002): http://europa.eu.int/comm/internal_market/en/company/company/modern/index.htm

The European Commission's Action Plan for Company Law and Corporate Governance (2003): http://europa.eu.int/eur-lex/en/com/cnc/2003/com2003_0284en01.pdf

The European Corporate Governance Institute http://www.ecgi.org

Revised Turnbull Guidance 2005 www.frc.org.uk/images/uploaded/documents

References

Barker, A (1997) *How to be a Better Decision Maker,* Kogan Page and The Industrial Society, London

The Combined Code on Corporate Governance (2003) Financial Reporting Council, London

Dunne, P (1999) 'What is an independent director?', in *The Independent Director: The role and contribution of non-executive directors,* The Institute of Directors and Kogan Page, London

Garratt, R (1996) *The Fish Rots from the Head,* HarperCollins, London

Gore-Brown, Sir Francis, Boyle, A J and Sykes, R (1986) *Gore-Browne on Companies,* Jordans, Bristol

Hamel, G (1999) *Gary Hamel on Strategy Innovation,* IIR, London

Handy, C (1978) *The Gods of Management: How they work and why they fail,* Souvenir Press, London

Haywood, R (1994) *Managing Your Reputation,* McGraw-Hill, Maidenhead

Institute of Directors, ed Tony Renton and John Watkinson, The Company Director's Guide, The Institute of Directors and Kogan Page, London.

Institute of Directors (2001) *Standards for the Board,* Institute of Directors and Kogan Page, London

Johnson, G and Scholes, K (1997) *Exploring Corporate Strategy: Text and cases,* Prentice Hall, Hemel Hempstead

Kalinauckas, P and King, H (1994) *Coaching: Realising the potential*, The Institute of Personnel and Development, London

Kaplan, R S and Norton, D P (1996) *The Balanced Scorecard*, Harvard Business School Press, Harvard, MA

Kendall, R (1998) *Risk Management for Executives*, Pitman, London

Parker, H (1990) *Letters to a New Chairman*, Director Publications, London

Porter, M E (1985) *Competitive Advantage*, Free Press, New York

Report of the Committee on the Financial Aspects of Corporate Governance: 'The Cadbury Report' (1992) Gee and Company, London

Sherman, M (1999) 'Making the most of your reputation', in ed Lesley Shutte, *Reputation Management: Strategies for protecting companies, their brands and their directors*, Director Publications, London

Sinclair, N, Vogel, D and Snowden, R (eds) (1997) *Company Directors: Law and liability*, FT Law & Tax, London

Sloan, A P (1986) *My Years with General Motors*, Penguin, Harmondsworth

Sworder, C (1995) 'Hearing the baby's cry: it's all in the thinking', in ed R Garratt, *Developing Strategic Thought*, McGraw-Hill, Maidenhead

Webley, S (1998) *Codes of Business Ethics: Why companies should develop them – and how*, The Institute of Business Ethics, London

Index